STORIES FROM A BROOKLYN STOOP

My Story Growing Up In Good Old Brooklyn, USA

STORIES FROM A BROOKLYN STOOP

My Story Growing Up In Good Old Brooklyn, USA

James C. DeLaura

All rights reserved by the author. This book may not be reproduced, in whole or in part, without the written permission of the author, except for the purpose of reviews.

Stories From A Brooklyn Stoop Copyright © 2019 by James C. DeLaura

ISBN: 9781087280714

To my wonderful and loving wife, sons and daughters-in-law.
You all have given me so much joy and satisfaction in my life.
Your encouragement and support made writing this book possible.
I will forever love you all and cherish our precious moments together.
Thank you for having faith in me.

TABLE OF CONTENTS

Dedication

Preface

Chapter 1   Introduction

Chapter 2   The Players

Chapter 3   The Early Years

Chapter 4   I Remember

Chapter 5   Trouble Was Our Middle Name

Chapter 6   Introduction To Making Money

Chapter 7   Never A Dull Moment

Chapter 8   The Ball Games

Chapter 9   Rules Of The Game

Chapter 10   Boy, How We Played

Chapter 11   Discovering Girls

Chapter 12   More Short Stories

Chapter 13   Learn While You Earn

Chapter 14   Brooklyn Street Smarts

Chapter 15   A Wonderful, Wonderful Adventure

Postscript

Acknowledgments

PREFACE

I am so grateful to have a vivid memory of the years I spent growing up in Brooklyn, New York. On many occasions, I've spoken with old friends and acquaintances about some of our experiences. Their recollections were typically vague and lacking in detail. The episodes and stories in the longest running serial I know of, my life, have since become even more important to me. It is as if I have become the historian of our youth.

Over thirty years ago, I met three friends I knew from the old neighborhood at three unrelated events within weeks of each other. The odds of this happening in such a short span of time seemed astronomical. I didn't realize it then, but those chance meetings became my inspiration to write this book. As you would expect, we talked about our families and jobs, but could not stop ourselves from reminiscing about our childhood days back in Brooklyn. Soon afterward, I wrote some notes about our experiences, then developed an outline to follow. Eventually, the needs of my growing family and the ever-increasing pressures of my career pulled me away from making any progress and my plans for the book were abandoned. In 2018, long since retired, I discovered my notes and outline in an old file box. So, at age 72, with renewed enthusiasm, I realized one of my life's dreams and finally wrote my book. I hope you enjoy reading it.

CHAPTER ONE

Introduction

INTRODUCTION

If you're one of the so-called "baby boomers" then, like me, you may have spent countless moments thinking back to your childhood when time went by in a more unnoticed and carefree fashion. Today, in contrast, we seem to measure time between the multitude of events and obligations in the course of our everyday lives. Like the workweek, or the time between paychecks or the monthly bills. Life, in general, is much faster than it ever was. For just a little while, I'd like to turn back the clock and be in good old Brooklyn, USA where I grew up and developed many memories to last a lifetime. Back then, Brooklyn was the world to me.

During the 1950s, our time was filled with an endless supply of friends, games and imagination. It seemed that whatever you wanted to play, there was always someone available to do it with. You could almost always play stoopball right in front of your house, or play one on one at basketball or stickball in the schoolyard. Team sports like baseball and football required a little more planning, but many other street games were played with regularity. Some of my favorites included punchball, slapball, and boxball. Today, much of the spontaneity of pick-up games is gone from our comfortable suburban neighborhoods. If the kids aren't being driven to an organized sport they're probably at home playing video games. Of course, there was school, but the minute we got home and changed our clothes, we were out on the street. The only caveat was to get home by supper – which was typically 6:00 pm on the dot. On rare occasions, you were a little late. I recall my mother yelling my name out from the kitchen window of our second-floor apartment. Boy, did I race home, up the stairs, all the while praying that my father wasn't already sitting at the table. In those days, the father was the head of the family, and for us, was truly the king of the castle. Crossing him was risky and could easily end up earning you a reprimand at the very least. Typically, some sort of punishment was given out when we misbehaved. Being late for supper was no exception. Although, most of the time, punishment was given out in proportion to the infraction. If a spanking wasn't in order, then you would certainly be vanquished to the stoop for an hour or so.

Many people living in the suburbs probably don't know what a stoop is. But if you're a city kid, it was second nature to you. The stoop was the last thing you would see when leaving your house and the first thing you would see when returning home. By definition, a stoop is the steps in front of a house. In most cases, the stoop consisted of from two to ten steps. Each step was deeper than your typical flight of steps, thereby making for a more comfortable seat for the stoop sitter.

It was a great place to converse with your friends, neighbors and family, play cards, listen to a ballgame on your transistor radio, and have lunch or a drink. The stoop was an ideal place for us during those warm summer nights prior to air-conditioning. Even as young children we knew we were not to wander off beyond the limits of our front yard. Besides, an adult always seemed to be in the area keeping an eye on things as they, too, enjoyed the evening. I remember catching fireflies that we called "lightning bugs" and placing them in an empty jar with air holes

James C. DeLaura

poked through the screw-on lid. Once we had a dozen or so inside the jar, we had our own lantern. Placing them into the jar was always a challenge as they all wanted to escape whenever the lid was opened to put yet another one inside. Just before we were sent to bed, we would release them.

So many of my memories took root on the stoop and most were good ones. However, the stoop had a dark side as well. When I was reprimanded for something or outright punished, my stoop was a lonely place for me. Many hours were spent sitting alone on the stoop as I was told not to move or talk to anyone. It was like an open-air detention cell. There always seemed to be adults around who would instinctively know that I was being punished and keep their distance. They would not allow their children to sit there and distract me from my penance. Once my time was up, everyone wanted to know what I did, especially if I had to sit there for a long time. In some ways, it was like going to confession with your friends. If you were in the confessional for a long time, or if you spent a lot of time in your pew praying, the guys would always want to know what you did that was so bad. For me, the stoop was central to my young life in Brooklyn. It was where my father bounced me on his knee as a young child, where I played stoopball or engaged in casual chatter. My stoop was where I sat in deep thought, or served penance for some childhood infraction. A stoop was the focal point years later, when I saw my beautiful future wife, Joanne, sitting on hers.

Looking back over the many photographs from my childhood, it was quite clear that the stoop was also a favorite place for many of the family poses. It seemed that every event or celebration in our family had been photographed there. Recalling memories from those days was a real inspiration for me to write this book. There are many stories I am lucky enough to still remember in great detail. Sharing them here is like reliving them for me. You may relate to some of these stories or just be amused by them. Some of them are quite silly while others are somewhat dramatic. We were all kids at one time; how nice it is to remember some of those years. It is really special to have good memories. Enjoy all of yours!

CHAPTER TWO

The Players

Every story has its characters and players. Mine is no different, with the players from my childhood deeply anchored in my memory as if they were still playing their parts in my early life story. Pouring over old family photos conjured up many images and stories for me. I wish there were more of them; we should all be able to cherish our roots.

PARENTS

First and foremost, and what surely must be the forge from which my character was shaped, was my parents. In the 1950s and 60's, my parents, like many in America, were raising their children with considerably less financial resources and buying-power than many today. But like most, did the best they could to make our lives better than theirs was growing up. My mother was one of the most kind-hearted women I ever knew. She exhibited her loving nature and simple approach to life every day. My mother was always there for her children while allowing us the freedom to be kids. She was the first person to go to when we had a problem. If my report card wasn't up to snuff, she would sign off for me, hoping my father was too busy to ask about it. While she covered for me, she encouraged me to do better and made sure I did my part before the next report card came out. I worked hard not to disappoint her and tried to do whatever she needed to have done around the house.

Even as an adolescent, I saw how hard she worked raising my two siblings and me. I would take on simple tasks like carrying the groceries, pushing the shopping cart or doing errands for her, which always made me feel good. Through all the years, my sister and brother also shared the same feelings and would do whatever they could for her. By far, my sister Lilly was a constant tower of support to our mother as an adolescent and when she became a mother herself.

My mother died when she was only 64 years old. We all took it very hard; it was and still represents the saddest time of my life. Like many people who are reminded of events in their lives by a song, a familiar place or perhaps the aroma of something cooking on the stove, I can still see

Stories From A Brooklyn Stoop

her face clearly. Whenever I hear some of the songs she loved, I always stop in my tracks and think of her. Like most mothers, she taught me many lessons. Being respectful of others was her Golden Rule. She said not to expect anything for the good deeds we do and the reward comes in the form of knowing you did the right thing. When in my early teens, she relayed a rather descriptive saying that she had heard from her parents, "If you spit in the air, it only falls back on your face." It left me with a vivid picture in my mind and probably saved me from many instances of hurting someone or embarrassing myself in the process.

My father was always busy and had less time for nurturing. This allowed, and actually encouraged us to fend for ourselves during our developing years. After teaching us to ride a bike, or catch and throw a ball, we were basically on our own to develop our skills in sports. In the summer, or when on vacation from school, we were out of the house almost all day, returning for meals, our favorite television shows, and some chores. About once a year, my father would take me to the large complex where he worked. It was exciting, passing through the buildings where he repaired and maintained machinery and equipment. While we would go directly to the workers' locker rooms, I remember seeing huge cranes and pulleys that moved heavy machinery in the distance. Once we got to his locker, he'd open it, reach in and pull out a large glass jar filled with pennies. My eyes would open wide as I knew they were all for me. For several years, it became "our thing to do." I remember opening the jar and placing the pennies in coin sleeves we got from our bank. Since I was never good at this, my mother would finish the job so we could cash the pennies in for dollars. Thinking back, the money I got back was probably how I started my baseball card collection, which was one of every boy's favorite hobbies back in the 1950's.

My father was like most fathers of the day, but as the eldest son in his family of nine brothers and sisters, he was the man to go to for advice and assistance. He never wavered from that informal role as his siblings or their children often sought his counsel. Even with his eighth-grade education, he seemed to have become a master mechanic, plumber, electrician and builder. He could do it

James C. DeLaura

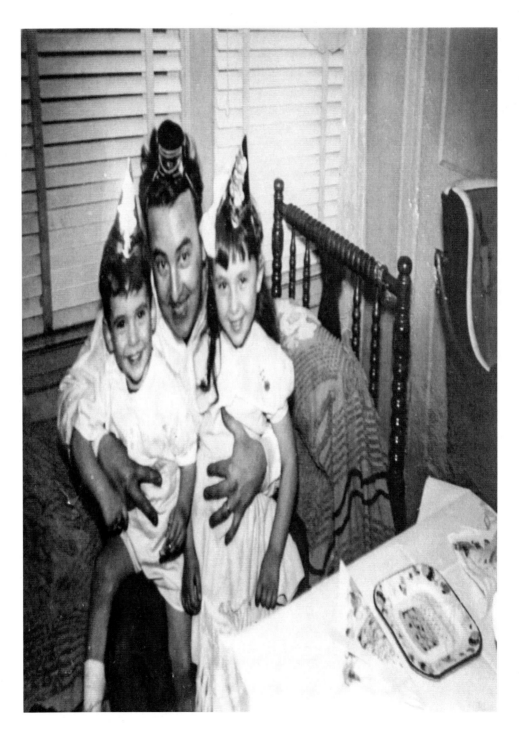

all and I wanted to be just like him. When I was with him, I realized that there was more to growing up than having fun or playing sports for me. His only fault in that regard was his tendency to be a perfectionist. I recall my mother's frustration with him when he started a simple project like painting our faded living room ceiling. Once he committed himself to the job, he meticulously opened up every crack in the ceiling using a pointed can opener. This step alone could take a few days to finish. By the following weekend, if nothing else pulled him away from the project, he would prepare a mixture of dry spackle, water and just the right amount of ceiling paint to ensure a better match with the final coat of paint. Making up small amounts of this mixture at a time, he'd climb up the ladder and put the first of several coats in the cracks. This process took several weeks to complete as he had to wait for each coat to dry, then be sanded, cleaned and made ready for the next coat of the patching mixture. I remember seeing the unfinished paint job sit for months as he went on to another project. To him, the real challenge was to repair the ceiling and achieve a permanent fix. Anyone could paint the ceiling, but only a craftsman knew how important it was to properly prepare. He eventually got to prime and paint the ceiling, which I know was a real chore for him.

    Whenever I could, I would stay close to him when he was doing something in case he needed me. He was a heavy smoker and often hacked away with his distinctive sounding cough, then only to light up another cigarette. I was always concerned that he would get a heart attack. Learning from him was not what you would call "On the Job Training." It was more like "Learning Through Intimidation 101." In the beginning, I was just a gofer. Jamie, as I was called as a young boy, get this, and Jamie get that. Sometimes, I had trouble knowing exactly what he wanted so I would bring him more tools and gadgets than he needed. My father would appear to be irritated and would shout something like, "Don't you know what a Stillson wrench is?" I'm sure the majority of people today have no idea what it is, but this ten-year-old had to know. When I eventually had a house of my own, much of what I learned came in very handy for me. His attention to detail and concern for proper preparation influenced me in many ways and was certainly one of the reasons I became an Engineer.

My father was also the family enforcer. As the eldest son, I typically bore the brunt of much of the punishment. Getting into trouble was no problem for my friends, cousins and me, so I seemed to be in the doghouse often. By today's standards, some of the treatments I received might be considered borderline child abuse. But that was so normal in the day that we never thought it was anything else but just treatment for getting into trouble or doing something you shouldn't have done.

It's sometimes strange how we see the people in our lives. As a kid, I thought my mother and father were always parents, born into it so to say. I don't recall thinking of them as having a life of their own before I came along. It wasn't until I was in my early teens that I recalled my parents talking about their youth and the years just prior to having children. Looking over some old family photos, it was clear that they did have a life before my siblings and I came along. It was great to see the pictures they had. It was a shame that these photos were kept in a box like some unseen collectibles, safely tucked away. This might be the reason why my wife and I have always framed

James C. DeLaura

and displayed family photos in our home. Most of our photos have been preserved in albums for us and the children to enjoy. Many of our memories are often relived as we look through these albums from time to time. Showing family photos on a computer or cell phone is nice, but it doesn't have the same effect as passing around our hard covered albums documenting the history of our family's growth. In any event, I love looking at the old photos of my parents, and find it amusing that at this point in my life, I too, now have "old" photos of my own.

GRANDPARENTS

My grandmother and grandfather were another story. They were both born in Italy and came to America like so many immigrants before and after them. They both had very hard lives, yet managed to buy their house in Brooklyn and raise their nine children. Raising children was quite different in those days as most of them were expected to go to work so they could contribute to the household. My father, for example, left school after the eighth grade to earn money for the family. As long as I can remember, right up to the passing of my grandparents, my father was always nearby to help them in any way he could. He was a good son, which made my siblings and me all the more grateful for what our parents gave us.

My grandmother seemed to always look the same for as long as I knew her. She was a sweet lady, strong as a bull, and always had a soft spot for her grandchildren. She always wore a loosely fitted housedress, and would typically have on some sort of apron. Her gray hair was always kept in a bun and she had one of those light-colored moles on her chin. At least once a week my grandmother would send me to the bakery to buy a loaf of "black bread". The first time I heard this expression, I thought it was some sort of stale bread she got at a discount. I later found out from my mother that it was actually whole wheat bread made in the same shape as a typical loaf of Italian bread. Whenever I ordered the black bread, I would get funny stares from other customers at the bakery. Eventually, I just asked for a loaf of whole wheat bread and always got what she wanted.

Another shopping experience I remember was when she would send me to buy "javel," which was a type of liquid bleach used for cleaning clothes. I'd walk up the street to a house with a wrought iron gate. Attached to the gate was a string, which when pulled, would summon an old woman from her second-floor apartment. She would open a window, stick out her head and ask what I wanted. I'd shout back that I wanted a gallon of javel. One of her grandsons would soon appear, take twenty-five cents from me and go to their nearby garage. He would use a large funnel to fill up a glass gallon jug with this pale-green colored liquid. It all was very interesting, but I have to say a bit intimidating for me. At about ten years old, waiting for that woman to appear was not a pleasant thing to do. Then, once I was given the gallon, I had to be very careful not to drop it. The whole chore was a mini nightmare for me. Thank God I didn't have to do that very often.

One of my father's brothers was a fruit and vegetable peddler, which meant he sold produce from his truck. Several times a week, he would replenish his stock at a large commercial market. He'd use my grandparent's backyard to store everything overnight. In the morning, large flat carts on wheels called dollies, full with boxes and bushels of fruits and vegetables were pulled out to the front street curb to be loaded on his truck. When loaded, the dolly probably weighed hundreds of pounds. I remember quite vividly seeing my grandmother grab hold of the rope that was tied to the front edge of these flat carts and pull them almost effortlessly out to the truck. In the evening when my uncle returned, the process would be reversed. The truck was unloaded and the boxes placed on those dollies. My uncle and grandmother again pulled them to the backyard where they would be covered with tarps until the next day.

Most of the time, my grandfather was nowhere to be found, or would be sitting somewhere close by to "keep an eye on things." His job came when it was time to recycle the empty wooden boxes. He'd spend hours dismantling the boxes that were no longer needed, banging at the ends of the wooden slats and pulling out the nails that held them together with the claw end of his old hammer. Sometimes, he'd let some of us use his hammer, but mostly we were there to pick up the nails and put them in empty coffee cans for future use. In those days, hardly anything was thrown away. Every now and then he would let my cousins

James C. DeLaura

and I take some of the salvaged wood and nails to make our swords and box scooters. It was always best to try to stay on my grandfather's good side. My grandfather was a small-framed man of very few words. I remember, he kept his hair in a crew-cut and maintained a thin-looking "pencil" mustache as he got older. His face was very wrinkled from all the years in the sun and he always seemed to have a gray, five-o'clock shadow on his face. My grandfather would sit for hours a day on one empty wooden crate while leaning his folded arms on another larger one. He would move about the block from one side of the street to the other with his wooden boxes. No one seemed to mind seeing this old man sitting in front of their house as if he lived there himself. I remember coming home from school and greeting him. He would then kiss me as he pressed his spiny beard against my cheek and sucked it at least two times. All of his grandchildren had to go through this ritual as pulling away would be disrespectful, so we would all just grin and bear it.

He spoke to us in his broken English, which at times, sounded quite funny. For example, he would pronounce

James C. DeLaura

Brooklyn as "Brook-a-leen," which always made us laugh. Whenever it was someone's birthday, my grandfather would sing the happy birthday song to them, except in his version, happy birthday sounded more like "after the birthday." We teased him about that but he just smiled at us.

Playing around the house was always a tricky thing. Since my grandfather was usually within the area, we'd have to treat him like a sleeping giant. If annoyed, he might yell at us, or more likely, chase us away. Back then, it didn't seem odd to us for him to do this, even though chasing your own grandchildren away would be unheard of today. In any event, many a report on my behavior was delivered to my father on his return home from work. Talk about real-time communication; my grandfather didn't need texting back then, he just waited for my father to come home to rat me out.

As I got a little older, but before my teens, my grandfather would use me to divert my grandmother's attention from him. Deep down I knew what he was doing, but I was glad to help him out. You see, my grandmother was always after him to stop smoking or drinking wine. If I went downstairs to visit them in their basement apartment, he would sometimes take me in the back to, as he would say, show me something. Of course, the moment we reached the rear of the basement, he'd light up a cigarette or pour himself a glass of red wine – sometimes both. Once done, he'd gesture to me as if to say, thanks for helping me get away with this grandson. I'd love it, for anytime he was happy, things were good.

MORE OF THE FAMILY

Like many married couples of the time, it was not uncommon to have more than five children. In our family, our paternal grandparents had five sons and four daughters. On our mother's side, our grandparents had three sons and four daughters. With one of our maternal grandparent's children marrying one of our paternal grandparent's children, we still had 15 aunts and 15 uncles as we were growing up.

Ever hear the expression, cousins by the dozens? Well, we had them. I believe the actual count was 34.

Whenever there was a reason to have a family get-together, the young cousins present had a great time, as we would typically be placed at our own table. Once the meal was over, we all dispersed outdoors for more fun together. Parents must have loved this as it cleared out the house for them. Adults were always present to keep an eye on things; the flow of people in and out of my grandparent's place seemed to go on all day long.

It's intriguing how many of the milestones in our family were memorialized in front of our stoops. For example, just about every wedding album has photos of the bride and groom posing with the rest of the wedding party on their stoop. This practice must have been seen by all as a very natural thing considering the similarity to the steps at a church. In the 1950's, my cousin Roslyn and I were the "flower girl" and "pillow boy" respectively, for our Aunt Jean and Uncle Louie's wedding. While my recollection of the event is a little vague, I do remember having loads of fun with my cousin and that it felt good to be fussed over.

Whenever my cousins and I received the sacraments of our faith, taking a photo on our stoop was also a common thing to do. Even as babies, when we were too young to pose, our parents had to have a picture taken with the stoop in the background. Looking through the family's old black and white photographs, the stoop always seemed to be the backdrop of choice for everyone. I suppose the stoop was not considered just a stone and concrete place to sit, it had become the family's place to come together and celebrate many of the good times in our lives. It's always been interesting to me how such a humble family custom became an important part of many of my early memories.

My cousin Jim and I were very close friends growing up. He was almost a year older than me so I looked up to him from the very beginning. We only lived a few blocks from each other so it was quite easy for us to do things together and, of course, get into trouble as well. Whether splitting a candy bar, planning to build a box scooter or sharing a First Communion photo opportunity, our grandparent's stoop always seemed the place to be. In the 1950's, we were practically inseparable as we both liked many of the same sports and activities. We were boy scouts together, loved setting up and playing with our electric trains and had a common interest in just about

James C. DeLaura

everything else kids did back then. It was great having a close friendship with my cousin. In my early teens, Jim seem to become my confidant once I discovered girls as I would frequently seek his advice in such matters. Through the years we always remained the best of cousins and to this day, share a mutual life-long friendship often fondly referring to each other as "cuz".

My other favorite cousin growing up was Roslyn, who was called Rozzie. When we were just starting out in school, we were so close that if either one of us didn't make it in, the other would cry for an hour. Until about ten years old, the family referred to us as "kissing cousins". Rozzie and I remained close friends throughout our teen years spending many hours on the stoop, playing with the family dog, Sandy, or at the beach in Coney Island. Today, we are good friends and love to talk about our youth.

While some of the family moved about the United States, most of us lived in Brooklyn. Many of my father's brothers and sisters actually lived within a few blocks of my grandparents. At one point, six of them lived within walking distance of their house. The interaction was great,

James C. DeLaura

but I have to say, it sometimes made for some strange bedfellows. Arguments and feuds cropped up now and then. It was difficult at times to know who my siblings and I could talk to. You see, in an Italian family, it was all about respect. If our father was on the outs with one of his brothers or sisters, then we were expected to avoid contact with them as well. As children, we didn't have a problem with this as we were in the category of seen but not heard, so it almost didn't matter. It became an issue when we were teenagers and young adults since we were raised to respect our elders, especially our aunts and uncles. Most of the time, we were able to find a way to keep our ties with all the relatives regardless of the feuding. Sooner or later, the feuding hatchets were buried and everyone kissed and made up just in time for another feud to begin.

FRIENDS AND NEIGHBORS

My friends were all unique characters. They had their strengths and weaknesses, which became common knowledge to one another. Whenever we would choose sides for a game, you can be assured these strengths and weaknesses were taken into consideration. Each team would start with the best player named as captain. Since every captain wanted to pick the best players, the rule of the day was to take turns selecting players for your team. It was always tough to be one of the weaker players as you were typically the last ones to be selected. Looking back, it didn't really matter to those players since just getting to play was the important thing. In those days, guys weren't concerned about hurt feelings. If you didn't get picked by one of the captains, you just had to grin and bear it and hope to play in the next game. There was so much interaction day in and day out that many of the friendships became long term ones, some even lifelong. Sharing stories from those days in Brooklyn has always been, and will always be, a cherished part of our lives.

A sure-fire way of meeting people in the neighborhood was simply to sit on your stoop. It was like being at a reviewing stand in a parade. Friends and neighbors would pass by giving a short hello or stopping for a longer chat. I always got a kick out of this one guy, Pete, who would walk past my grandparent's house the same time almost every day. As he passed, he would shout out something in Italian only to have my grandfather respond with his one word reply. In all the years this went on, I don't recall a time where Pete actually stopped to talk to my grandfather, just shouted out his one-liner, waved his hand, and kept walking. There was some rhythm to it all.

NICKNAMES

Some of the guys had nicknames, many of which you won't hear much of these days. Yes, you might hear someone referred to by his two initials like TJ, but nothing referring to a physical feature of the person. This would be neither nice to do nor be politically correct today. However, back then it all seemed acceptable to everyone, including the person given the nickname. Some of the nicknames that come to mind of friends and older guys in the neighborhood were Tiny, Chubs, Skee Ball, Red, Monk, and the Turk. There was also this skinny kid who talked all the time. He would rant on and on about what was going on or what had happened in the neighborhood. My cousin Jimmy and I nicknamed him, "News in a Nut Shell." Sometimes, we'd just call him "News" to keep it simple. How something like this came about beats me, but the expression means to sum something up in a few words. While News would keep his updates short, they never seemed to end, so I guess the nickname just worked for him.

The best friend in my life is my buddy, Jim. Sharing much in our lives since we were about fourteen, we came up with an odd nickname for each other that has stuck to us like glue for over 50 years. The where, when, and why this name came to be – neither of us can say. But one day, we heard a word used that we thought was Italian, only to later find out it's actually considered more of a Brooklyn-ism than Italian. The word is "Shongod" and it means someone who's messed up. We both seemed to like the way it sounded and to this day will still greet each other with an enthusiastic, "Shongod!"

Jim still reminds me of a time when his grandmother, who spoke almost no English, would only acknowledge me as Shongod. He laughs as he recounts the story where she asked who was at the door of her house one day. He told her, it's my friend, Jim. Looking confused, she said in Italian, chi è, which means who is it?

He then said, Shongod, and she looked up with a smile and said, ah, Shongod! What he doesn't realize, is that because there are several Jim's in our circle of friends, everyone in my family knows him as "Jimmy Shongod" to this day.

Besides the uniqueness of nicknames, the origin of first names is interesting. Growing up, it was customary for my father and his brothers to name their first son after my grandfather. As you might expect, this resulted in a lot of male cousins with the same first name. Handling this was no problem as each of us named James was called by some variation of the name itself. The eldest was called Jimmy. When I arrived, I was called Jamie, and the next was called Jimmy Boy. After the first few brothers did this, the two younger ones chose to break off from tradition and named their first-born sons after themselves. Although no one spoke of it at the time, we were all relieved that we didn't have two more cousins named James in the family.

Besides your relatives and friends, the other players were all the neighborhood vendors, shopkeepers and service people. Back then, these folks knew your first name and you knew theirs. People took the time to talk to one another and there was a bond between them.

TALK ABOUT A MELTING POT

Everyone knows that New York City is referred to as a melting pot of cultures, nationalities, religions, sexual orientation and ethnic backgrounds. Our Brooklyn neighborhood was no different; there were all kinds of Italians there. They hailed from every corner of Italy. The old-timers could make a pretty good guess where someone was from by the dialect they spoke, or even from their last names. Speaking of dialects, if you were from New York City, Brooklyn in particular, you probably had a distinct accent. Brooklynese, as it was called, was easy to pick up by any outsiders. A dead giveaway is the dropped "r" sound in some words like boid (bird) or woik (work). Using dis for this and dees for these is also very common. For me, living in the suburbs of New Jersey for over 35 years, has toned down this accent. Nevertheless, my New York sound is undeniable. It's funny how people react to the subject of accents. For example, back in the 1970's, I attended a weeklong conference in South Carolina. At a luncheon with some local colleagues, the subject of accents came up. I made mention of their southern accent, which caused the group to erupt into laughter. They said, Jim, you're the one with the accent. They were correct, after all, I was the one standing out like a "saw dumb".

There was a sizable Jewish population where I grew up. Everyone seemed to get along very well, family values were very similar and the kids intermingled through school and sports. One of my good friends, Alan, was Jewish. I remember he would love to go out for pizza but also enjoyed a nice pastrami on rye now and then. He probably should be credited for introducing me to the Jewish Deli. What great stuff we'd get at the deli; like frankfurters, potato knishes, matzah ball soup and cream soda. One time I asked for beans with my frankfurter, except I ordered pork and beans. Alan had to tug on my arm to get my attention, and then explained to me that's a no-no in a Jewish Deli. My face turned beet red with embarrassment. The deli man said something to his co-worker then looked at me with a half-smile as I tried to correct my order. It was quite a while before I went back there, but I couldn't resist those yummy knishes.

THE BULLIES

Every neighborhood had its share of bullies. Back then, we called them "tough guys." The trick to survival in the neighborhood was either to avoid them at all costs or buddy up with them. In reality, neither strategy worked for me. Avoiding contact with them was easier said than done as they could be almost anywhere at any time. And there was no way I could ever be considered a buddy to any of these guys. One time, as I walked along the avenue, I was roughed up by a group of tough guys just because one of them knew a friend of mine that they didn't like.

One day, a friend of mine asked one of the neighborhood tough guys to work out with us. The workout session was to be in my basement as I had the only workout bench. On the day of the workout, I purposely let everyone in through the back door so as not to alarm my mother. Our new friend was a few years older than us, and his sheer size would definitely disturb her, to say the least. We were all in awe of him as he went through a short workout with us. His massive arms and chest just blew us all away. As he loaded the barbell with weights, it became

James C. DeLaura

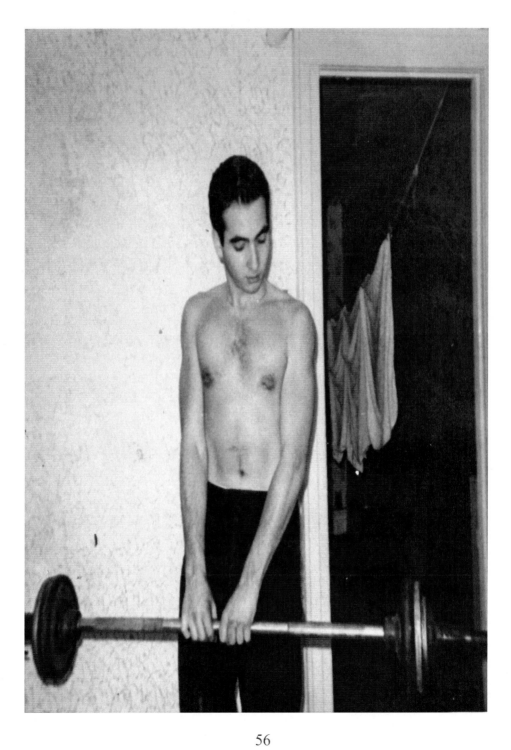

evident that we didn't have enough on hand for him to do his usual routine. He seemed to go through his exercises with ease as he explained the proper breathing techniques, handgrips and stance to use. It was quite an education and a whole lot of fun. We all tried hard to impress him with our lifting ability and muscles. Shirtless, my puny upper body revealed a little definition but I struggled to impress him with some heavy weights that I tried to lift.

He seemed like a nice guy to take the time and give us some workout tips. After that experience, whenever we saw him, he'd give us a wink or a thumbs-up sign, which despite his reputation, made us feel pretty good. A few years later, I learned that he was killed in some incident and I felt really bad. Unfortunately for some of the tough guys, they drifted into relationships with the wrong elements in my Brooklyn neighborhood. The stark reality of the criminal world touched us even at our young age whenever we'd read about a fatal shooting or stabbing and realized it was one of the so-called neighborhood tough guys.

CHAPTER THREE

The Early Years

On the day I began writing this book, I thought to myself how nice it is to be able to reach back in time and recall the early days of my life. There really isn't anything unique about that I thought, after all, we all have "early days". Later, talking with some friends, I could see a sparkle in their eyes or a smile come to their faces as they listened to one of my stories. I couldn't help think that, while listening to me, they were going back in their own minds and recalling their own early-day stories. As they shared some of their stories with me I experienced that same sparkle or smile.

However, some of these episodes from our past weren't always pleasant or upbeat. While it is human nature for one generation to strive to improve the conditions of their children, for many, the process can be a long, arduous one. Like most parents, mine made do with the money my Dad brought in. It's interesting to note that, according to the US Census Bureau, in 1950, the average family income in the United States was $3,300 per year. In 1960 it was $5,620. Even though the cost of living was much lower than today, it was a wonder that they were able to provide for us as well as they did.

NO PLACE LIKE HOME

Growing up in a small three-room apartment with your parents, an older sister and younger brother meant there wasn't much room to move around, never mind play in your own room. In fact, none of us had our own room as they were shared by all. This arrangement was especially hard on my sister, even with a makeshift privacy blanket hanging down the center of the bedroom that my siblings and I shared. She had her own bed on one side and my brother and I had a bunk bed on the other side. There wasn't enough space in the room to put much more than a clothes bureau, and the one closet we had was packed with family stuff. It was a difficult situation for all of us, but again, when we were very young, we really didn't know what we were missing. However, it wasn't until I was much older that I realized how hard my parents really had it. Their bedroom, without a door for privacy, doubled as our living room. We would all gather around the console that housed the family radio and listen to our favorite shows.

Later, when we got our first black and white television set, we would again gather around to watch the shows we were allowed to see. There weren't that many choices back then, but who cared, we had a TV!

BLASTING OFF

I remember our apartment's living room quite clearly. As I said, it actually served as our parent's bedroom and the family's living room. There was my parent's bed, dresser, a couple of chairs, cedar chest, large radio console, and, when we could finally afford it, a black and white television was added. The cabinet housing the radio was huge and resembled a chest of drawers. Some sort of mesh-covered the large speakers in the center of the unit. Above the speakers was a glass-covered dialing system. The tuning display was very large with tuning, volume control and power knobs located just below the station indicator. For me, it became the control panel of my make-believe spaceship. I'd pull up one of our chairs and spend hours at the controls. Then, I'd zoom around the universe like one of my heroes. There I would play, sitting in front of the control panel with my father's 1940's vintage radio headset, and my toy ray gun that sparked when the trigger was pulled. Methodically turning each dial and knob as I adjusted my altitude, speed and direction, I would start a new adventure. Sometimes, my parents would scold me, and rightly so, for fear that I would certainly break something. Eventually, they were convinced I wasn't abusing the privilege so I was left to my imaginary missions without further concern.

During the Christmas holiday, that room was the center of activity. We wrapped our presents and decorated our Christmas tree there. It was also where I'd set up my electric trains. I remember one year my father brought home a piece of plywood that we painted green to simulate grass and, in no time, it became the layout board for my trains. I would play with them for about two weeks before they'd be stored for the next year. Storing the board was a snap as it would go under my parent's mattress to help stiffen it to help with Dad's back problems. This room was a far cry from the spacious living rooms, dens and family rooms many of us take for granted today, but it was the most versatile room there ever was for us back then.

Our one bathroom always seemed to be occupied by

James C. DeLaura

one of us. When we were young kids it was just bearable. Once we reached our teens, the conditions became quite the opposite. I recall those days all too well, when we would all jockey for our own "bathroom time." Thank God, our grandmother's apartment was just two flights of stairs away in case of emergencies. Nevertheless, we seemed to manage, but still couldn't wait for our parents to purchase our first house. I do recall, with some humor, the times when my father was outside the door, shouting, "Come on, did you fall in?" Once they did buy the house, the days of being rushed out of the bathroom with a desperate pounding on the door became a distant memory.

Our kitchen was also an extremely versatile room. Not only was it the place where my mother prepared our meals, but also where she bathed us as infants, washed and ironed our clothes, and paid the bills. It was where my father did his paperwork and met visitors. It was also the place where we did our homework or just hung around.

We had an old-fashioned, wringer type washing machine that sat near the sink so it could be connected to the faucet for water and the sink for draining. To one side of the sink was our dryer. Well, I mean the window to

James C. DeLaura

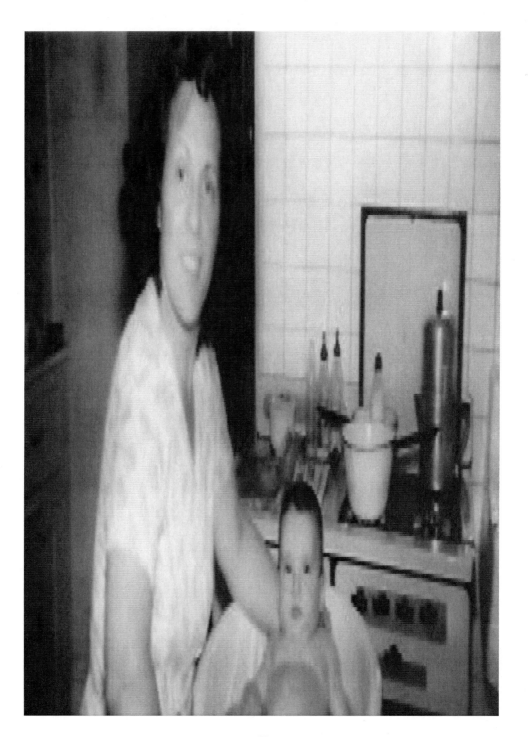

reach the old clothesline. From our second floor apartment, my father attached a pulley to the house and strung a clothesline to another pulley on a pole in the backyard. It was always funny for us to see our clothes hanging on that line, and I suppose it was just as funny to some of our neighbors.

Doing laundry really had to be hard on my mother. It was a chore just to hook up the water supply, wash the clothes, wring them out and drain the dirty water. On top of that, she had to hang up the wash on the clothesline, item by item, with wooden clothespins. The whole chore was particularly difficult in cold weather when the laundry froze up. Pulling in the dried, I mean frozen, clothing, towels and sheets was a sight to see. Certain pieces of laundry resembled the frozen codfish (called baccala) sold at local markets. Whenever my mother pulled it in, she referred to it as pulling in the baccala and we would all laugh at the sight. Then we'd all help her place the frozen laundry on our beds to thaw out.

When I was sixteen, my parents bought their house and I thought I'd finally get my own room. But that just wasn't the case. My assigned bedroom was at the very front of the house and was really the sitting room for the family during the day. I had a high riser type of bed so the sleeping area was covered during the day and used as a couch. There was no privacy as the room was situated at the front of the home's railroad room configuration. When I was in my late teens, if I came home in the wee hours of the morning, my father would come in to check on me. Emerging from his bedroom at the other side of the house, I'd see the flicker of a match as he lit up a cigarette and went into the bathroom.

When he came out, he walked slowly in total darkness towards my room. I could see the tiny glow from his lit cigarette heading towards me and braced myself as I pretended to be asleep. Through my squinting eyes, I watched as he approached my bed. It was as though he was on a slow train traveling through the night with its single headlight lighting the way towards me. Once he reached the foot of the bed, he'd fumble along, then finally feel his way to my toes hidden beneath my blanket. He was just checking to see if his son was home safe. I always got a kick out of that and loved him all the more for it.

James C. DeLaura

SADDLE UP

My other favorite place to play while at home was at the end of my parent's bed. I'd use the small post on the footboard as my saddle horn pretending to be some cowboy on the range. Once we got our first black and white TV, my world of superheroes grew and grew. Of course, back then, they weren't called superheroes, just "good guys." Dressed in my cowboy hat, holster and six-shooter, I would pretend to ride alongside my old west heroes. I'd spend countless hours galloping along the range as I sat at the edge of that bed. My father would let me use one of his belts now and then so I had stirrups to keep me from falling off my imaginary horse. Yes, that small room served a lot of our needs and, for us, was a true "living room".

CEREAL WARS

We grew up with the simple things in life, like having corn flakes or oatmeal for breakfast almost every day. That's why my sister and I appreciated the times our mother treated us to a variety pack of cereals. As soon as we got the box home, we would divvy up the cereals. Since my brother was much younger than we were, he was not cut in. Then, we'd toss a coin to see who would pick first. We then took turns selecting our favorite cereals until we had five boxes each. With all our boxes selected, we might consider trading one box for another. Then, came the most important step, which was to put our initials on our boxes – establishing ownership. We'd place the cereals in the pantry, my sister's on one side and mine on the other.

The next day, we would place all our boxes on the table in front of us, making a pile so we couldn't see each other while we ate our cereal. I'd always try to knock down her pile of cereal boxes and, of course, she would cry out to our mother. The result was predictable, as I would always be reprimanded. Nevertheless, it was a barrel of laughs for both of us. Many years ago, I bought a variety pack of cereal while grocery shopping with my wife. For laughs, we wrote our initials on the boxes. Wouldn't you know it, my wife and I fought over the selections just as my sister and I had done as children back in Brooklyn!

WHAT'S A BROTHER TO DO?

Teasing your sister was what brothers did when they were ten years old. I was no different. In fact, I developed some unique ways to tease and pester my sister back then. One of my favorites was my "corn teeth routine." My sister, Lilly, would never admit it, but I think she actually liked it. If our dinner included some corn, I'd sometimes put a spoonful of kernels in my mouth, then gesture to my sister to slap me on my cheek (not too hard of course). If she did, I pretended that some of my teeth were knocked out and began spitting out corn kernels one by one into my open hands. It wasn't as disgusting as it sounds, rather funny I thought. My parents didn't approve, never laughed, and always asked me if I would ever grow up. Still, to this day, the cereal box and the corn teeth stories make my sister and I laugh whenever we think back to our young Brooklyn days.

KEEP THOSE FEET CLEAN

One of the hazards of roaming about the neighborhood's empty lots was stepping on nails, glass or other discarded materials. I stepped on my share of nails in those pre-teen years. The first time it happened to me, I remember making the painful trip back home where I would seek the comfort of my mother. She always knew what to do in such matters. Cleaning out the wound with hydrogen peroxide, she showed little mercy for the stinging sensation I would experience. She would put on some Mercurochrome and a bandage. Then came the reprimand, as my feet were far from clean. She said, that's why I should always have clean feet. You never know when you might get hurt and have to bare your feet to someone. I didn't think much of her comments at the time as I was in considerable discomfort and just wanted to feel better.

After getting lectured about why I shouldn't play in the lots, she called the doctor's office. Concerned that the nail was rusty, we went to the doctor to get a tetanus shot. That seemed to hurt almost as much as the nail puncture. Now, I was protected from future complications of stepping on rusty nails. Keeping my feet clean all the time was another matter that I didn't give much attention to; after all, I was a kid.

TREES DO GROW IN BROOKLYN

Over the years, many people unfamiliar with Brooklyn would see it as city-like in the same way New York City surely is. But, for those of us living in Brooklyn and the other Boroughs, we only consider New York City (Manhattan), as the City. We have trees almost everywhere. Parks are abundant; as are gardens, beaches and shorelines. When I was a boy, my backyard had a few fruit trees and grapevines that were available to us throughout the summer. I can almost taste the juicy peaches and figs from our trees. Our neighbor's apricot tree was a treat for us. Since the large tree limbs hung over a chain-link fence and into an empty lot, we never felt bad about snapping ripe ones off to our delight. The grapevines in my grandparents' backyard flourished and it was always fun to pick the grapes right off the vine. We'd suck the juice from inside the white grapes, then discard the thick skin.

All of the shade trees were always sources of fun for us. We'd use small twigs for making miniature huts and forts when we played with our toy soldiers or cowboy and Indian figures. If we came upon maple trees, we were sure to find "samaras," which was the official name for the fruit of the maple tree. Some referred to them as "helicopters" because they would whirl around like a helicopter's rotors as they fell to the ground. Many others, including my cousins, friends and I, called them "polynoses." Once these winged samaras floated to the ground, we'd pick them up, open one, and place it on the tip of our nose. The sticky substance inside allowed us to hold it in place. And there you had it, a polynose! As silly as it sounds, we would keep them on for quite some time, often competing to see who had one on the longest.

Stories From A Brooklyn Stoop

CHAPTER FOUR

I Remember

We all have stories of our past experiences but many of us leave it to others to tell their own stories instead. When I started writing this book, I would share one or two of my experiences with a friend or family member. When I did, they seemed to have an urgency to share a story of their own with me in return. Their stories were usually very funny and I often wished I had lived them myself. So here are some of mine that may trigger your good memories of interesting times in your own life.

CHRISTMAS TREE TIME

Once summer vacation ended, it was back to school. But before you knew it, Halloween was here and Thanksgiving followed. By then we all knew it was really getting close to Christmas. It's funny how we seemed to remember holidays as milestones in our lives back then. Today, and what seems like for the past twenty-five years, retailers everywhere have taken charge of the holidays. I don't mean this literally, but let's face it – as soon as one holiday is upon us, they're displaying their wares for the next one. For example, chocolate Easter eggs were being sold at the same time Valentine's Day candy was prominently displayed at a local drug store in my neighborhood. Artificial Christmas trees and lawn ornaments go on sale at big box stores right after Labor Day. It seems like these retailers want to beat the competition to the marketplace and the poor consumer gets caught in the middle. As a boy in Brooklyn, Christmas enjoyed its own spotlight. Leftovers from Thanksgiving were long gone and there wasn't a trace of a pilgrim or turkey ornament to be found.

It was a great time of the year - we got a vacation from school and received gifts too! The season was all-abuzz with good cheer about family, friends, and celebrating the birth of Christ. There was no Black Friday to kick off a shopping frenzy after Thanksgiving Day. Shopping for Christmas presents was a simple and easy process since most families had a limited budget for gifts. Our presents were modest ones, maybe one or two at most. A small army jeep and truck set for me, an old west fort complete with cowboy and Indian figures for my brother, and perhaps a new doll and clothes for my sister were well appreciated. This was a far cry from the gifts of today where most of us spend hundreds and even thousands of dollars on them for family and friends. For my family, as finances got better each year, so did the gifts.

So it was with our Christmas tree. In those days, nearly all trees were real fresh-cut trees, not artificial ones. When I was about eleven years old, my parents entrusted me with buying our tree. Not something you would imagine a kid doing today. The day before Christmas Eve, my father gave me a whopping $3.00 to buy "the best tree I could get". Since nice Christmas trees would cost a lot more especially when they were first brought in, the strategy was to wait until December 23 to buy one. Even back then, getting a nice tree for $3.00 was practically impossible. The task was daunting for an eleven-year-old but I was determined to make the family proud of me and bring home a nice tree.

A few weeks before Christmas, the trees were set up along a main street, under the elevated trains. All the vendor needed was access to a power source to get the lights up and running as most of their business was done in the evening as folks returned from work. Ordinary light bulbs were strung between makeshift poles placed in the ground much like the way circus tent poles would be supported. Several old garbage cans with holes punched through them were placed inside the compound. These garbage cans held mostly discarded pieces of tree branches and scrap wood that the vendor would burn to warm up the area. What a great Christmas season aroma these pieces of pine gave off. No one was concerned about air pollution or a fire hazard back then, just selling trees.

The Christmas trees would be placed in rows supported by crude rope fences. The whole scene seemed magical to me. I arrived before dark and looked through the entire stock of trees. Even at this late stage, there were still a large number of trees available. Deliveries of trees seemed to take place several times a week up to Christmas Day. I skipped over the pricier trees and concentrated on the cheaper ones. Taking a tree out from where it leaned on the rope fence, I would turn it around so I could see it from all angles. Once I found a nice one with a bare spot or broken branch, I'd put it back with the imperfection well exposed, then I went into action. I told the guy that my father had given me $3.00 to buy a tree. I really want to get

Stories From A Brooklyn Stoop

a nice one but it doesn't look like I have enough for it. This one here is $8.00, but it has a large bare spot. See! Can I have it for $3.00? At this point, the guy was probably thinking it's the day before Christmas Eve and there's still a lot of trees left. This one probably won't sell so why not give it to this kid for three bucks?

It worked like a charm and I was off with a pretty nice tree for a decent price. Once home, I helped my father make a wooden base to fit the tree and place it in our living room ready for the family to decorate. The tree looked great with its bare spot hidden against the wall. Everyone was very pleased with my choice and my father was glad I got such a nice tree for the $3.00 he gave me. Looking back, I can say this was my first experience with the art of making a deal, coming many years before Donald Trump wrote a book about it.

AIN'T NOTHING LIKE MY MOTHER'S COOKING

I've been really blessed when it comes to family cooking. My wife and sister are great cooks and have made many delicious dishes over the years. But when it comes to memories of my youth, my mother's cooking comes in first place. Some of my favorite dishes include her veal scaloppine, beef stew, veal and peppers, spaghetti and crabs, peppers and eggs, chicken soup, mashed potatoes, macaroni and cheese, icebox cake and my favorite – lemon meringue pie. But the best was her tomato sauce, which, to most Italians was called "gravy". It wasn't at all like beef or turkey gravy, but it was a rich tomato sauce heavy with the juices of the meats she simmered into her saucepot.

The pot was as old as the hills and only used for her gravy - I think it added to the flavor if not the ambiance, of the whole experience.

Hot and sweet Italian sausage, pieces of pork, and her fabulous meatballs were placed in a skillet with oil and garlic. She would lightly sauté the mixture then add it to her sauce inside that large pot. Sometimes as a treat for the family, she would make some bracioles and add them to the gravy. Bracioles start out with a piece of beef pounded into sheets as thin as today's sandwich wraps. Then she would roll the sheet adding seasoned breadcrumbs, pignoli (pine) nuts and softened raisins.

James C. DeLaura

Tying the rolled-up delicacies with some string, she would place them into the pot. After a short while, you could see the oils from the meats rising along the rim of the pot. She would gently stir the pot revealing the different meats as she did so. Sometimes, I would do the stirring for her with anticipation of digging in later. As soon as she asked me to get the Italian bread at the local bakery, I knew we were getting close to dinner. Our neighborhood bakery made great Italian bread, pastries, and delicious donuts. Once back home, my mother would reward me by letting me sample the gravy. She'd cut a small sliver of bread from the end of the loaf called the heel. Then, I'd stick a fork into the end and just touch the surface of the simmering gravy, trying to sop up as much as I could without losing the bread into the pot. A little cooling off, then pop into my mouth — it was so good.

Earlier that morning, my father would send me to buy a large bottle of soda at the candy store. This was the only day of the week we were allowed to have soda so it was great to be able to pick out my favorite flavor. The owner was a good friend of my father so he'd allow me to get my own bottle from his icebox. This was a large chest with a lid that opened much like a storage trunk. It was full of quart bottles of soda surrounded by ice and water. I'd roll up my sleeves and reach into the box, digging down until I found either cream or cherry soda. Today, no kid would ever cherish putting his arm into a sea of ice and water to pick out a soda bottle, but in those days I thought this was the best twenty-five cents ever spent.

WOULDN'T TOUCH THE STUFF

Sometimes we had "delicacies" – as defined by my father – that I wouldn't touch with a ten-foot pole. The memorable thing about these dishes is the total disgust I had for them. Take "Capuzzelle" or roasted sheep's head (please). On a night that my father seemed to skip supper, he would later show up carrying a brown paper bag. The first time we saw this mysterious bag soaked with oil we gathered around him in anticipation as he sat at the table. We all hoped there were zeppoles inside. Zeppoles are deep-fried dough balls about 3 to 4 inches in diameter. It is like a doughnut that's topped with powdered sugar. When placed in a bag, the oil would soak through the paper as this one did. Once he opened the bag, we ran away from the table as fast as we could. You see, it was capuzzelle, and we saw it up-close and personal. With the bag opened, there seemed to be no time to waste as he picked the meat off the sheep's face with a small fork. We were all horrified and must have had nightmares that night. After that time, whenever my father came home with an oily paper bag we ran for the hills.

When I was in Junior High School my mother would ask me to stop at a butcher shop on my way home. It was always to pick up something simple, like chopped meat, but every once in a while she wanted me to get some cow's brains or tongue. *Why couldn't it be frankfurters or hamburgers?* I would think to myself. Well, my father liked scrambled brains and eggs every now and then — yuck!

SNAIL RACES

The neighborhood was always filled with small shops that would exhibit their goods and wares on the sidewalk just outside their store. I suppose it was their way of advertising what they had for sale. The neighborhood fruit and vegetable market was no exception. They would place loaded bushels and crates under a cloth awning in front of the store. People would walk by and check out what was a good buy that day, then go inside and make their purchases. Oddly, one of their top attractions was live snails. I remember how they would be contained in an open wicker-type basket on the sidewalk. Every so often, some of the snails managed to work their way up to the top of the basket and fall, or crawl, their way to the ground. Once this happened, we felt that they were fair game and would pick them up and take them home. If we had three or four of these critters, we would each pick out our favorites and race them down a makeshift course in someone's backyard. Sometimes, the race would take so long that we'd become bored with it all and bring them back to the store in disgust. None of us could ever understand why someone would buy these things, but later found out that they are a delicacy when prepared properly. Still, to us, they were just slimy slugs with shells.

CHICKEN MARKET CHICKEN

If there was one place I hated, it was the local chicken market. As a young boy, I was horrified to see the goings-on there. I can still remember the first time I went there with my mother to pick up a fresh chicken. Up until then, I didn't understand what the term "fresh" meant when used in the phrase "fresh chicken." I soon found out that it meant "fresh-killed." There was no fanfare, just place your order, then watch the slaughter right before your eyes. I suppose this was second nature to the adults, but the horror of seeing a chicken stripped of its feathers in plain sight of all of us made me sick. If that wasn't enough to traumatize a kid, at the other end of the market, one of the butchers was skinning a rabbit that was hung on a steel hook over a long stainless steel trough. The chicken market's pungent smell permeated the whole place and was disgusting. This was certainly not one of the more pleasant memories of my Brooklyn boyhood, and the chicken market image stayed with me for a very long time. Some years later, I was elated when our chickens were bought at the neighborhood food market where seeing the word "fresh" just meant, freshly packaged.

James C. DeLaura

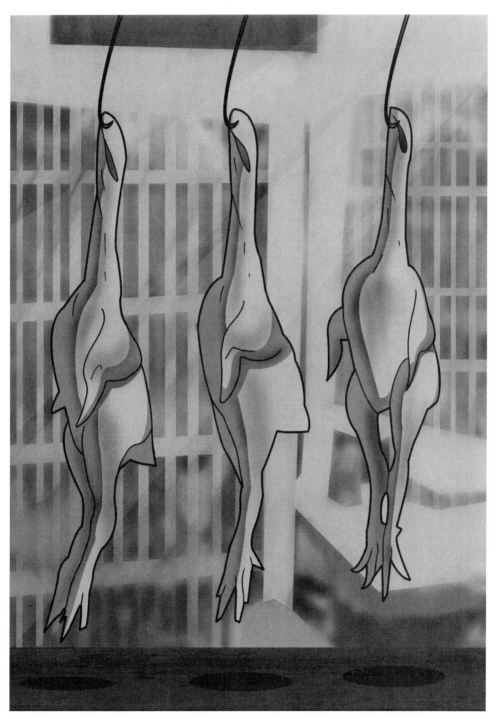

SANDY, THE FAMILY DOG

My uncle found an abandoned Cocker Spaniel puppy at the produce market where he bought his fruit and vegetables. Like all the boxes and crates that he brought to my grandparent's house, he brought home the puppy as well. In no time, the puppy became part of the family. He belonged to all of us – grandparents, aunts, uncles, and cousins. We named him Sandy because of his sandy-colored coat.

All of us played as much as we could with Sandy, but over time, he seemed to gravitate to my grandfather. While my grandfather didn't play with Sandy, there was this bond that made them nearly inseparable during the day. Sandy, who was never on a leash when with my grandfather, would follow him up and down the block all day long. When I returned from school, there was my grandfather, sitting on his wooden box with Sandy at his side. Since Sandy was an outdoor dog, he slept in an insulated doghouse that my father made for him. Sometimes, Sandy would prefer to sleep near the back door to my grandparent's house under the covered part of the yard

James C. DeLaura

that we called the shed.

Thinking back, he was always a healthy dog and it was amazing how well he developed, eating only the leftover food that comprised his diet. Being owned by an Italian family meant that Sandy had a steady diet of vegetables, baked ziti, pasta fasulli (pasta and beans), meatballs and sometimes sausage. Everyone brought Sandy a "doggie bag" whenever they went out to eat. For example, every time we went out for Chinese food, my father would collect all the leftovers into one plate and have the waiter make him a doggie bag to take to Sandy. Onetime, we urged my father to request two bags; one was for the doggie and one for us. I wanted to enjoy what was left of my roast pork lo mein the next day and couldn't fathom eating it mixed with my sister's chicken chow mein. Either way, Sandy gobbled up whatever was brought to him.

Over the years, my cousin Rozzie and I developed a strong attachment to Sandy and became his caretakers in the same way our grandfather was his daily companion. We were close cousins back then, and practically inseparable during our early years. It was only natural that we had the same feelings about Sandy and shared the joy he gave us. We'd walk him often on a leash and took care of his grooming and bathing. There was nothing like the unconditional love this dog gave us. When we called his name as we returned home from school, he'd leave our grandfather's side and run to us, licking and jumping with joy. I remember when Rozzie and I would save up some of our own money to buy Sandy real dog food, a commodity the family just couldn't afford to do. Rozzie lived down the block from me, so on the day we bought the dog food, we would meet at our grandparents' back yard so we could feed Sandy. Once opened, the canned dog food smelled much like uncooked corned beef hash, although we would never think of tasting it to confirm that. As we opened the can, Sandy's small nub of a tail wagged wildly. He would gobble up the food as we were spooning it into his bowl. To him, the experience must have been intoxicating, because whenever we bought another can and showed it to him, it set off that little wagging tail again. It was as if he began to salivate by the mere sight of the can. We loved it. To this day, whenever I open a can of corned beef hash and get that distinctive aroma, I can almost relive those wonderful days with Sandy.

Rozzie and I knew that as Sandy got older, his roaming privileges would be curtailed and he had to have his leash on all the time. He began to growl and bark at people, and our grandparents were losing their patience with him. We tried to spend more time taking care of him, but it was almost impossible with school and homework. Since I lived upstairs in my grandparent's house, I would usually stop by the backyard to see Sandy, even if for only ten minutes or so. One day, I couldn't find him so I left the area and went about my business. Going back after dinner, he was still nowhere to be found. Finally asking my grandmother where he was, she said, "We had to put him to sleep." I was horrified and immediately ran down the block to Rozzie's house to tell her what I just learned. We were both in tears and went back to see our grandmother to see if there was anything that could be done. It was too late, Sandy was taken away from us, and a piece of both Rozzie and I was gone forever. We tried to convince ourselves that it was all part of growing up. Over the years we would bring up the fun times we had with Sandy, but that always left off with a bittersweet feeling.

James C. DeLaura

THE DEEP SIX

The slang phrase, "give it the deep six," was typically used by seamen and meant to get rid of something into the sea. My father taught me what it meant, and what I was to do when he said it. Something unusual for a ten-year-old to understand or even know about. For me, it meant to cut up a small stack of paper my father had given to me into small pieces and flush them down the toilet. I never asked why, it was a simple chore and I felt I was helping him out. I must have done a good job as he always said, "Atta boy," after he saw how I followed his instructions to the letter. When I asked what the little papers were for, I was told it was a game he and his friends played. I don't recall how long I did this chore, but it didn't seem that long. Maybe it was a passing fancy for him, but I never thought much of it. Many years later as a young adult, I heard the words, "deep six," once again and questioned my father about the times I'd cut up those pieces of paper for him. It became clear to me that it was related to a very common form of gambling in the 1950's. People would bet on a combination of three numbers and the expression, "hitting the number," was a phrase often heard in the neighborhood. Thinking back when I was a boy, I suppose my father's explanation was totally understandable. Actually, I was giving the "deep six" to the remnants of the nickel and dime bets he made on the numbers he liked.

AND THEY'RE OFF

Like many of his time, my father loved horse racing. My first introduction to the "sport of kings" as it is called, came one spring day when talk of a big race was all-abuzz. As I sat on my stoop amongst my father and some of my uncles, I would listen to them discussing the race coming up that Saturday. They'd discuss the odds, favorites, long shots, jockeys and trainers. I sat still on the stoop that day in the hopes of not being shooed away. While I didn't understand all of the terms they used, it was fun to listen in.

At the age of twelve, I started the eighth grade at our local Junior High School, which was located about a mile or so from my house. Sometimes, my father would ask me to stop at a particular candy store on my walk home from school to buy him a newspaper. It wasn't one of the well-known daily newspapers; it was a horse racing paper. The paper had all the statistics on the horses running at various tracks and was a must-have tool for someone trying to handicap a race. I sometimes wondered why the vendor never hesitated to sell the paper to me, a twelve-year-old kid. I do remember getting some heads turning from the men hanging around the store when I asked for it. Once my father returned from work, he'd study that paper for information on the horses racing at his favorite track.

The most vivid memories of my father's racing hobby has to be the times he would listen to the race results as I came home for supper. I would run up the flight of steps to our second-floor apartment, and upon entering I'd shout, "I'm home," only to hear my father yell back at me, "shut up." My mother would follow with, "Quiet, your father is listening to the radio." Then, I'd hear the voice of the race announcer shouting, "And they're off," which meant, of course, he was listening to the race he had bet on. I always hoped he won so he'd be in a really good mood at supper. On the other hand, he never showed any anger if he lost – but winning was always better. While this was not the norm in my house, it always makes me laugh thinking back to those times. My father and I sometimes joked about it when the topic came up later in life. Some thirty years later, my wife and I took him to a racetrack in New Jersey for a pleasant family outing. As we sat at one of the outdoor tables, he was all about business. He studied the handicapper's sheets and the past performances of the horses racing that day. As soon as my wife and I started up a conversation with him, he would look up at us and say, "Shoosh." While my wife was obviously annoyed, all I could do was smile as I thought to myself that nothing had changed in all those years.

PITCHING QUARTERS

Many Sunday afternoons were spent in and around the stoop in front of our house. Since my grandparents lived there, most of my aunts, uncles and cousins would flock there to spend time with them, as it was essentially our "family day". Inside the house, it was usually a chaotic scene with chairs seeming to appear from thin air and filling all of the empty spaces in the kitchen and living room. Food was everywhere as some of us were eating dinner, while others came by for dessert, or just to say hello. It was a glorious time; I loved seeing everybody, especially my cousins. As soon as we were allowed to leave the house, we'd immediately disappear into the yard or on the front steps to play stoopball or some other game. Since we were dressed up in our best Sunday clothes, the games had to be more sedate and less rowdy than usual. God forbid we got those clothes dirty or tore something. A scraped knee could be tolerated, but never a ripped pair of pants.

If the weather was nice, all my uncles would eventually gather in front of the stoop and pitch quarters against the bottom step or some nearby wall along the house. The game was simple, but it sure got them all excited as the competition got underway. Each of them took turns pitching a quarter towards the step or wall. Basically, whoever pitched the quarter closest to the wall won all of the quarters played. Boy, there were some close calls and that was when the fireworks started. There always seemed to be an argument amongst the players and then some kibitzing from the other adults watching the game. Kibitzing comes from a Yiddish term describing someone giving unwanted advice or comments while watching a game or other activity. I recall there was a lot of kibitzing going on when my uncles got together - it was something all the cousins looked forward to. It was all clean fun and each of the cousins rooted for their father to win. I remember having to retrieve the quarters for my father when he won. Sometimes, he'd give one to me as a sort of tip. We all couldn't wait for our turn to play such games. When some of us got together, we played "pitching pennies," a much more affordable game for us.

HUNDRED POINTS

Playing cards was infectious for most guys while growing up. If we weren't playing ball, we could easily play one of several card games for hours, or until called away by our parents. Games such as war, brisk, and rummy were some of our favorites. Poker came along in our later teens as we honed our skills playing with plastic chips or small amounts of money. I also vividly remember playing rummy and 500 rummy with my mother on many winter afternoons. She loved those games and was very good at them. My mother was a good teacher and I still play the games today with my wife.

But I can't seem to shake off the memories of my

early teen days playing rummy with my neighbor. When the family moved into our first house, we met our neighbor John, an elderly man with a distinct Eastern European accent. On the day we moved in, he greeted us and asked where we were from, then wanted to know if any of us played rummy. I later found out how much he really loved playing the games. It seemed a little odd, but it was a real passion for him. Once in a while, he and I would play rummy in the backyard. He wouldn't talk much, except when it was pertinent to the game. I was okay with that, as he was a very serious man – actually very intimidating. When he did speak, however, it was if I was speaking with Dracula himself. His distinct accent sometimes ran chills down my spine. Still, it was rather fun for me.

After playing many games with John over the course of several weeks, it was obvious that I was a formidable opponent even as a young teenager. In fact, I would win more games than he did. This would frustrate the heck out of him. Eventually, John resorted to a pre-game ritual that was actually pretty disgusting to me. Before each deal, he would shout out, "hundred points," in his Dracula voice, then spit lightly into his hands and rub them vigorously as if he was washing them with soap and water. Unfortunately for me, it was with his saliva. Yuck, I would think to myself. His ritual really didn't make a difference as I continued to beat him regularly. I have to admit, my concentration sometimes wandered as I contemplated the next game and John's hundred points ritual. After about a year of playing with him, my studies and part-time jobs prevented me from continuing our regular games. To this day, the thought of that expression conjures up some unsavory memories for me. Nevertheless, when playing cards with my adult children I sometimes find myself using John's expression, including the accent, but without the spit of course.

DINNER TABLE MEMORIES

After we moved into our new house, my sister, Lilly, would bring her boyfriend, Larry, over for Sunday dinner from time to time. It was interesting to watch the dynamics of the family and how each of us reacted to this new visitor. For me, I rather enjoyed the attention Larry gave to all of us. My mother and father were treated with the utmost respect. I remember that he would shower my mother with compliments about her cooking, which we all unanimously agreed with. It was my father's reaction that was the main attraction for all of us. We knew he wouldn't be comfortable with anyone that courted his daughter and we were ready for almost anything.

My father was known for his practice of taking votes on people. I guess he may have watched too many ancient Rome movies. It was just some family silliness where a person's acceptability in the family circle was voted on. Today, it would be quite rude to do such a thing, but back then it was sort of a fun thing, especially since we all were allowed to vote. I remember one of the first candidates was an aunt of mine who rented the apartment above us. She was my mother's sister and we would vote on her at almost every dinner that she shared with us. My poor aunt would always get the thumbs down from my father, but we all gave her the thumbs up. The whole thing seemed harmless and everyone, including the person being voted on, never took it seriously. I'm sure none of us, including my father, even knew what it really meant.

Once Larry became a regular at our house, voting on him was inevitable. At times, I even found myself voting

Stories From A Brooklyn Stoop

thumbs down, probably to gain my father's favor. However, as time went on, and Lilly and Larry's relationship got more serious, even my father would give his thumbs up. Still, Larry wasn't going to get off the hook that easy. You see, besides my mother's Sunday gravy, he loved her lentil soup. Of course, my father couldn't resist explaining to him that it was all in the stuffing that my mother used in the lentils. I suppose the guy didn't want to antagonize my father so he seemed to accept the story. Months later we all had a good laugh when the air was cleared about the stuffing of the lentils, which was an obvious absurdity. Nevertheless, the damage was done so even after they were married, my father often referred to him as, "Stuffed Lentils."

When I started to date my future wife, Joanne, I shared the voting stories and warned her what to expect. This never sat well with her and I fully understood. Before having her over for dinner, I asked my father not to engage in any voting. Even though I knew he would do it anyway, I felt it was worth a shot. Eventually, Joanne was sitting at that same dinner table where the family voted on my aunt and future brother-in-law. I was a nervous wreck, as I already knew Joanne didn't think much of the voting practice. It didn't take long before my father brought up the need to take a vote on her. Glancing at her, I could see she was struggling to remain calm, which she did with a smile that could melt ice. My father led off the vote with what looked like a thumbs down, caught sight of Joanne's face and, with a circling motion, stopped at a thumbs-up vote position. While relieved at the outcome, I later caught hell from her for participating in the vote at all.

THE ULTIMATE BROOKLYNISM

Growing up in Brooklyn, it would be almost impossible to forget the expressions used in the old neighborhood. Some of them were so catchy that they still show up now and then in today's vernacular. You even hear some of these expressions on television and in the movies. There has been much written about these expressions and an Internet search will provide interested readers with a plethora of information on the subject. However, for me, the joy lies in the fact that some of the terms and expressions were a part of my everyday language during my youth. It's amazing how some of these expressions are embraced by young people when they are exposed to them. Every now and then, one of these Brooklynisms slips out of my mouth and the reaction is almost universal - widening of the eyes and a smile on the person's face. Instantly, my Brooklyn roots are revealed, usually to the delight of those in earshot of the conversation.

Here are ten of my favorite expressions that I still find myself (and others) using. Maybe they'll become some of yours as well.

- Agita: An Italian word for heartburn or a feeling of agitation.

- Flat leaver: A friend who leaves you or breaks a plan when another friend or opportunity comes along.

- Gavone: Someone with crude manners or is said to eat too much.

- Haya Dooin: A greeting – how are you doing?

- Not-For-Nuttin: A term used to soften the impact of telling someone the truth that might otherwise be too offensive.

- Scutch: Someone being a pest or annoyance.
- Skeeve: Something that disgusts you, or grosses you out.
- Skinny Belink: A really skinny person.
- Weisenheimer: A smart-aleck or wiseguy.
- Yooz: Slang for "you". Yooz guys when referring to a group.

For me, the ultimate Brooklynism has to be "Fuhgeddaboudit" (forget about it). This phrase can take on different meanings simply by changing your inflections when speaking. Let's say you're discussing the food at a particular restaurant. If asked how's the food, you might say, "Fuhgeddaboudit" very quickly with a frown on your face and a downward hand motion. This would mean the food wasn't that good. On the other hand, if the food was very good, you could say, "Fuhgeddaboudit" slowly. There might be a smile on your face and the hand motion would be upward, possibly touching your lips, with a slight kiss of your fingers. Without these oral clues and hand gestures, the meaning of the statement might not be too clear and would precipitate another question like, "What do you mean?"

Even politicians recognized this Brooklyn expression. For example, in 2004, the Borough President's office authorized the erection of a highway sign that was clearly visible to drivers as they left Brooklyn at the Verrazano-Narrows Bridge for Staten Island. For many, the sign that read, "Leaving Brooklyn: Fuhgeddaboudit" was a memorable reminder of the uniqueness that is Brooklyn.

Stories From A Brooklyn Stoop

> **Leaving Brooklyn**
>
> **Fuhgeddaboutdit**
>
> Marty Markowitz   Michael R. Bloomberg
> Borough President   Mayor

CHAPTER FIVE

Trouble Was Our Middle Name

One thing the kids in the neighborhood had in common was our middle name, "Trouble," and we never needed any help getting into it. In those days, getting into trouble may have been fun and all too easy to do, but getting out of it, well, that's another story.

ALL TIED UP

It was just another ordinary day in my grandparent's backyard, so a couple of my cousins and I decided to do some play-acting with a mock burning at the stake. Of course, there was never any intention of actually setting anything on fire. As mischievous as we could get, we never played with matches as that would result in a punishment of biblical proportions. So there we were, with one of my cousins pounding on a makeshift drum while I began to coil a braided rope around another cousin's body. Starting at his legs, I just about reached his waist as one of my uncles suddenly appeared outside the side door of the house. Imagine the expression on his face when he saw the three of us. He was nearly hysterical as he yelled at us, "Stop! What the hell are you doing?"

Well, as you would guess, it wasn't a pretty sight. We were all hauled off into the house and had to explain to our parents why we would do such a thing. As the eldest of the three, I was scolded by every adult in the room. Even my grandmother, in her broken English, said I was, "a stupida." My father looked at me in disbelief, then marched me upstairs to where we lived. It was interesting to see my cousins grinning from ear to ear during the inquisition as I admitted that the whole thing was my idea. On the way up the steps, my father didn't say a word. When we entered the apartment, he pointed to the bedroom and said, "Okay, now assume the position." Assume the position was an expression, probably coined by my father, and meant, lie face down on the bed while I use a belt on your behind. Talk about child abuse! But again, in those days it seemed like the punishment fit the offense. Looking back, it was more symbolic than painful. A few whacks and it was over, well, at least until the next time I was, "a stupida."

THE GREATEST WHIPPER

Opportunities to showcase our ability to get into

trouble seemed to pop up out of thin air. Watching one of the variety shows on TV gave some of us the idea to try our hand at the use of a whip. The first step was to sneak one of my father's leather belts out from his closet. Then, two of my cousins would take turns holding a wooden stick loosely in their hands. We started out with a long stick and worked our way down to a piece about two inches long. I'd stand about three feet away and whip the stick out of their hands with the belt. Crack went the belt as the wooden stick was slapped from their grasp. The two boys really thought I was great at this when I cleanly hit the stick without touching their small fingers. I instantly earned the title, "The Greatest Whipper."

After many repetitions, the game began to get boring for us so I would give them the belt to use. They were terrible, repeatedly hitting me on my hand and arm. It seemed that their inability to master the technique made my reputation even greater in their eyes. One day, a cousin asked if I could whip a flat popsicle stick from his mouth. Okay, I said, and to everyone's amazement, I knocked out the stick with the belt cleanly. With my reputation intact, we played on until I finally missed my target and hit one of my cousins square on his head. Crying all the way into the house, he didn't hesitate to rat me out when questioned how this happened. And yes, I got punished once again. It was funny that the belt used to knock out the sticks from my cousin's hand was the same one used on my behind. After the pain subsided, I thought to myself that it was worth it to be known as the "Greatest Whipper," even if for only a short time.

CARPET GUN CRAZIES

Just about the craziest thing we did as kids was to make a carpet gun and then wage mock wars against each other. Thinking back, we were very lucky that we didn't blind one another. With all the wood we had at our disposal from my uncle's fruit and vegetable business, we would pick out a sturdy piece for the barrel of the gun. We'd cut it down to about two feet long and attach a strong rubber band to it about two-thirds of the way down the barrel. Pulling on the rubber band, we would test how far back we could go. Then we secured a wooden clothespin to the barrel, again pulling back the rubber band and locked it in the jaw of the clothespin. In those days, discarded pieces of linoleum were easy to get a hold of. Our parents rarely threw anything away if they thought it might come in handy. I remember finding rolls of scrap linoleum in my grandparents shed where just about anything could be found. We would cut off enough linoleum to load our guns and disappear into one of the lots to play. Next, we would place a small piece of linoleum tile (that we referred to as carpet) inside the stretched rubber band, aimed and released the clothespin. The piece of carpet would fly through the air with great speed toward its target.

We started out shooting at objects, such as a stack of tin cans, but soon escalated to choosing up sides and having carpet gun wars. Things got out of hand very quickly and guys were getting hit all over their bodies causing cuts and welts. Better judgment finally prevailed and we stopped the war games and we went back to just using the guns for target shooting. Even at that, there was always the occasional accident when the rubber band broke or the piece of carpet missed its target and hit some bystander. It was inevitable that we destroyed the guns and made peace. Of course, we were then on to our next mischievous experience. Slingshots anybody?

James C. DeLaura

DIRT BOMB FIGHTS

During the 1950's and 60's, development was booming in our neighborhood. Once the construction of a new house or row of houses began, bulldozers and other construction equipment would soon show up at the site. Within weeks, we had yet another field of adventure. The excavated hole for the foundation made a wonderful place to scale walls and pretend we were soldiers out on maneuvers. Soon after, we discovered an endless supply of compacted pieces of dirt. Some of these were small like a rubber ball while other pieces were much larger, but could be broken down into smaller sizes. Someone noted that they resembled hand grenades and so our game of army maneuvers took on a different nature. Let's play war! We would break up these clumps and make what we called "dirt bombs." These dirt bombs were hurled at each other as we pretended to be opposing armies at war. There weren't any rules, no time limits, we simply played until we were bored or the construction crew chased us away. Thinking back, we were fortunate again that no serious injuries occurred. However, one time, a dirt bomb hit me in the middle of my forehead and, unfortunately for me, contained a small stone. The impact and consequent pain was something I'll never forget. That incident caused us all to cease-fire for a while, or until we found another excavation. Explaining the open gash to my mother was interesting. To this day I cannot recall what reason I gave her, but I'm sure it was not a believable one – they never were.

THE COOKIE CAPER

This less than smart moment from my pre-teen years actually taught me a life-long lesson in diplomacy. During one of the countless days at my grandparent's house, one of my aunts had made a batch of cookies and asked if I wanted one. What kid turns down the offer of a cookie? So, I took one from the plate and started eating it much to my aunt's pleasure. "Yum yum," I said as I struggled to swallow down my first bite. It tasted much like a ginger snap, which is about the only cookie I didn't like. You see, I just couldn't say the cookie tasted horrible and hurt her feelings, so I did the gentlemanly thing and lied.

Somehow, I got it down without grimacing and took a

James C. DeLaura

second, smaller bite. I then tried to make a quick exit so I wouldn't have to eat the rest of the cookie. Much to my dismay, my aunt handed me two more cookies (for the road) as I left. Once outside of the house, I spit out the remaining morsel of cookie that I had lodged in my cheek, then I threw the remaining cookies away, flinging them like Frisbees into the empty lot next to the house. Holy cow, when I turned around there stood my aunt! I wasn't sure if her face was as red as mine, but it sure seemed to be. Then she said, "If you didn't like my cookies, you should not have taken more of them just to throw them away."

While I said I was sorry, she was clearly insulted and hurt. One lesson I learned that day was how to say, "no thank you." It would have been a lot better to say that than to have to apologize for an insensitive action. I don't believe I ever got another cookie from her, although it seemed that she eventually forgot about the incident, but I never did. Of course, the other lesson I learned was never to eat another ginger snap.

James C. DeLaura

SIXTY-CENT LUNCH

At eleven years old, having fun on a rainy Saturday afternoon might be lunch at our favorite Chinese restaurant and a movie matinee at one of the neighborhood movie theaters. We could do it all for under a dollar if we skipped the movie candy. It all started out with the sixty-cent lunch special at the restaurant. Looking back at our Chinese food lunches, we were probably the waiter's worst nightmare. Ten or twelve boys showing up at lunchtime with the intention of spending no more than sixty-cents for soup and chicken chow mein, noodles, duck sauce, tea, and a fortune cookie. We took up two or three tables and, once seated, the fun would begin. Some of the guys moved their seats so often that the waiters had to move plates from table to table. Others would ask for Italian bread and butter, while others gulped water down like crazy, keeping the waiters busy with refills. About the only thing we didn't do was have a food fight, which we knew would result in an immediate ejection from the restaurant and make it difficult to return in the future.

When it came time to pay the bill, all of us would go up to the cashier's stand located adjacent to the front door. Guys would be huddled closely, with one or two of us overflowing out the door, especially as new diners arrived. It was a chaotic scene and I'm sure the manager couldn't wait until we all left. We never agreed with the waiter's headcount and by the time they did a recount, some of us were long gone. We always managed to get through it all somehow, giving the waiter whatever we had leftover for a well-deserved tip. With our bellies full, we'd go over to the theater to watch a movie. All this for just under a dollar; how good was that?

MR. JOE'S WINE CELLAR

Mr. Joe was an eighty-year-old man who lived by himself in a house about a block away from my grandmother's place. He'd mostly sit on a worn-out seat pad that he'd place on the lowest step of his small concrete stoop. Most times he would simply sit there by himself, sometimes beckoning a few of us to sit with him. Needing not much conversation, Mr. Joe seemed fairly content to just have two or three of us around him for a while. He always wore a flat, checkered cap that he called a "Coppola" in Italian. Sometimes he would remove the cap to dry off his bald head with one of the dirtiest looking handkerchiefs we ever saw. Once the cap was put down to dry out, one of us would move to a step just above where Mr. Joe sat and begin to play make-believe drums atop his head with our index fingers. All the while uttering sounds meant to imitate a real drum. By the way, to this day, I have no explanation why we would do this.

Mr. Joe would tolerate this playfulness for a little while, then shout out the Italian phrase, "ancora" which means "again." I suppose that it was his way of saying, you got away with it once, but try it again and watch out! After one, or two more "ancoras," we knew his patience had grown extremely thin. We would then position ourselves on the stoop so we could leap off and escape his grasp. We'd then leave Mr. Joe's place and move onto our next adventure. After a week or so, we would pass his stoop again, always say hello and only approach him if he asked us to do so. It was great. Even though we were being total asses the week before, Mr. Joe forgave us or forgot about it altogether. Either way, we were his friends again.

One day, he wanted to take a few of us down to his cellar where he had made his own wine years before. While looking at each other with our eyes opened wide, we all thought the same thing; is this where he gets even with us for all our shenanigans? As none of us wanted to be the first to "chicken out," we all went with him. We weren't taken in through the front door; rather he led us to his front gate, then through the side entrance of the house. It was dark when we first entered his small stuffy home. The staircase to the cellar was directly to the left of us as we entered. Mr. Joe flipped a switch at the top of the stairs and a single light bulb went on, dimly lighting the way down. As you would expect, the steps creaked like some old castle staircase as we descended into his mildew smelling cellar. More lights were turned on and the cellar no longer looked as sinister as we imagined it would. Mr. Joe laid out some empty jelly jars on an old wooden table. He proceeded to pour red wine into each jar, filling his to the top while putting about one finger full in each of ours. He toasted something in Italian and we all drank. Mr. Joe swigged down his glassful and we all coughed as the wine went down our throats. Today, the mere suggestion of taking children into your house unsupervised would be against the law. The book would probably be thrown at someone who gave them alcohol as well.

But no harm, just some kids tasting an old man's wine. We made his day and probably his year. We never did tell anyone about it and Mr. Joe never invited us down to his cellar again. We stopped annoying him after that; just saying, "Hello Mr. Joe," when we passed him at his house. Several months later we stopped seeing him on his stoop and soon found out that he had passed away. We all felt sad and missed seeing him. We realized then that we should have behaved better when sitting with him and learned a lesson to respect our elders. To this day, whenever I hear the expression "ancora," I think fondly of Mr. Joe.

CHAPTER SIX

Introduction To Making Money

As young children, the need to have money wasn't something on our minds every day. Our parents provided the basic necessities; we didn't break it down further than that. Who thought or even knew about rent or insurance payments? We knew that if we wanted something, such as a pack of baseball cards or a milkshake, we'd need to have the money to do so. In my case, asking my parents was never a sure thing. In fact, unless there was some sort of holiday or birthday coming up, I didn't even bother to ask. Collecting empty soda bottles to turn in for their deposit money earned us some loose change but never really amounted to much. One of the earliest ways in which I made money was by running errands. Payment for these services was not well defined, and in most cases, was based on the "keep the change" system if I had to buy something for someone. After a while, the person sending me on the errand would seem to give me just the right amount of money to pay for that loaf of bread or bottle of soda. As I found other ways of making some money, I was less interested in running errands and only did it for my mother or grandmother, at no charge of course.

Coming up with new ideas for making money as kids

was just plain fun to do. We never had any pressure to make money, rather, it was something to do especially during those lazy summer days. One of the more common ways that seems to have survived throughout the years, is the old lemonade stand. I really get a kick out of seeing some kids selling lemonade in front of their house. Regardless how it might taste, I never miss an opportunity to buy a cupful of the stuff. I often wish I was a kid in this day and age with the popularity of bottled water. Boy, would I make a killing. Back in the 1950's, the mere thought of someone selling water would have resulted in a "who are you kidding" response.

One of the more creative ways we made some money during the summer was to put on a variety show in someone's spacious backyard. As long as our mothers and some neighbors were willing to sit through our amateurish production, we could easily make a dollar each for our efforts. I say mothers because our fathers were either at work or too tired to endure sitting through the event. While I have vague memories of the shows we put on, I clearly recall our collective efforts in pulling it all together. Even back then, it seemed my interests were more in ticket sales and the actual production than playing a part on stage. Probably an early sign that I enjoyed managing things.

THE "CAN SYSTEM"

I remember that my first real introduction to money management came about a year later when my mother showed me her can system. The concept was simple enough for me to understand. My father went to work, brought home money, and gave most of it (I assume) to my mother. She then put various amounts into each of five or six old cans that she had labeled: Food, Rent, Insurance, and so on. I clearly remember the cans – they were made of tin and resembled today's beer can, but slightly taller and more slender. They were rather colorful but never intended for display, as they were always kept well hidden in one of her dresser drawers. Each payday, the ritual was repeated and when it came time to pay a bill, she simply went to the appropriate can and made a withdrawal. It was like her own ATM.

Most business was done on a real-time basis back then. Well, not exactly like today where a utility company automatically debits their payment from your checking account. Real-time back then meant the salesman or representative came to your house and was paid on the spot. As if it was yesterday, I can see Joe the life insurance man making his rounds on my block. He would park his car and emerge from it with a huge leather-bound book that seemed to be at least a foot thick. A large shiny zipper that kept the book securely closed was clearly visible as Joe lumbered up our street to his next client. When he arrived at our house, I remember running up our stoop, ringing the bell to our second-floor apartment to alert my mother yelling, "The insurance man is here." She would then go to her cans and take the money needed to pay the month's installment. I believe it was about fifty-cents or a dollar at most.

Joe would have to walk up the stoop, then up the steps to our apartment with his heavy book. Noticeably out of breath, he entered the apartment, sat down at our kitchen table, unzipped his book and ran his finger down the right side to find our name. He then flipped the page to the left, and ran his finger down the page until he located the right box. Here, he would put a little check mark to indicate the appropriate monthly payment was made. The whole process took less than five minutes before Joe would close the book, zip it up and leave for another client's monthly payment.

That was the day I saw my mother's "can system" in operation for the first time and got my first taste of budgeting. I don't recall her referring to it as budgeting, but I understood then that if you wanted something, you needed to save up for it. It was also the day I watched Joe lumber through our neighborhood with his heavy book when I realized that I would never want to be a door-to-door insurance salesman.

YO, BAN-NAN-O'S

At the age of eleven, I got my first real job. My parents allowed me to work on my Uncle Danny's fruit and vegetable truck during the months when I was on summer vacation. Most kids between 14 and 17 that wanted to get a job had to get their "working papers" from the Department of Labor. At eleven years old you weren't allowed to work at all, but working with my uncle was evidently exempt from this law. Anyway, who was I to ask? I suppose my

interest in the fruit truck began several years before when I was about 7 years old. From the photo, it looks like I already had a hand in it. Usually, I would work two or three days a week. My cousin Jimmy and I would work every other day that correlated with two different routes his father would take. I wanted to work alongside my cousin, but my uncle knew better. The workday was long, starting out around 7:00 am at my grandparent's house. We had to help load the truck with the boxes of fruits and vegetables stored in their covered backyard. I remember the boxes had to be placed in a very precise manner on the truck. My uncle would create a tiered effect so all of the boxes and baskets were easily visible to his customers standing on the sidewalk.

Besides helping with the loading and unloading, and waiting on customers when needed, I had to keep the truck displays neat looking throughout the day. I was paid a whole $2.00 and picked up about a dollar more in tips if I was asked to deliver to a customer's home. I'd love watching my uncle in action and always looked forward to his call as we reached each of his stops. Once he got out of his truck, he would shout, "Yo, Ban-Nan-O's," at the top of his lungs. Surrounded by his fruits and vegetables, my uncle seemed like the king of the jungle as he shouted out to his customers. After they came out of their homes, he'd tried to tantalize them into buying stuff not necessarily on their shopping list. If cherries were in that day, he'd say, "Dear, I have some nice sweet cherries today," then give them a sample to try. They seemed to buy whatever they sampled. I also liked the way he held his pencil and would try to emulate him by holding mine between my ear and my head, but it kept falling off.

I was amazed at how he added up the bill for each customer. Most items had to be weighed on a scale that was hung where his truck cab was connected to the bed of the truck. As he weighed each item he'd calculate the price in his head then write down the amount on an unopened brown paper bag. Then all the items were added up with great speed, with the bag essentially becoming the customer's receipt. He had gained the trust of his customers from years of good relationships and apparently good fruit and vegetables. No one ever questioned him and probably felt they were always getting a good deal in the process.

THE JUNIOR SALESMAN

Just before the holidays, I took up selling mail-order greeting cards to earn prizes. My customers were mainly relatives and friends of my parents in the neighborhood. Strangers encountered by door-to-door selling would always say, "Not interested," then abruptly close the door in my face. As a result, my door-to-door selling days were very short-lived. Selling cards led me to eventually sell other products, like wrapping paper and novelty salt and pepper shakers from the supplier. It felt great when my prizes arrived, but after the first or second round of orders placed by my aunts and uncles, my selling days seemed to be over. After all, how many Santa spoon rests can one family want?

Later on, during my days in the Boy Scouts, I collected can labels for camping related prizes, like mess kits and canteens. While I never had much interest in my mother's grocery shopping list, I suddenly developed a craving for pork and beans, suggesting we put them on her list each week. She cooperated for a while but decided to cut down once she saw about a dozen unlabeled tin cans in her pantry. You don't think I was going to wait weeks on end to send in these precious labels, did you? No sir, I removed the labels and wrote "Pork and Beans" on the can. By the time my father stepped in to shut down the practice, I had my fill of pork and beans anyway.

CHAPTER SEVEN

Never A Dull Moment

Whether playing ball, riding your bicycle, skating, or playing a whole host of games, we never had a dull moment. If we didn't have a ball in our hands it might be a water pistol, a yo-yo, or a cigar box full of baseball cards. When we were in the presence of our parents, we were often told to just sit still on the stoop, a concept we found hard to understand. Stepping outside of our houses, or taking a short walk down the block, we could find someone to play with. Something was always going on by one group or another, so going out to play was like ordering food in a restaurant, just look at the menu and pick what you wanted.

LOTS AND LOTS

Schoolyards were great places to play ball games. Baserunning versions were played depending on the court size and/or the number of players we had. Empty areas called "lots" were found all over our neighborhood. A lot was an open area, sometimes located at the end of a block or between two houses or buildings. These spaces were left undeveloped for many years. When situated at the end of a block, people would use it as a shortcut to round a corner. As a result, these areas were fairly flat and clear, making for fields of play, our "fields of imagination".

Over time, we gave names to our favorite lots so we could differentiate them from one another. Each name seemed to take on one or more characteristics of the lot or its surroundings. For example, there was the "Jungle Lot," so named for its thick vegetation and harsh terrain. While ballgames could not be played there, we'd ride our bikes along trails we made throughout the Jungle Lot and set up clearings to meet, usually to play cards or just hang out. It was one of our favorite places to get away. Every so often, some of the older kids joined us in a large open area and would make a small campfire to roast marshmallows or even potatoes. There was no recipe to roasting potatoes; we simply placed them into the fire and embers where they cooked. When we thought they were done, we used a stick or twig to pull them out and tested them. Once done, the totally blackened potato skin was peeled back as we ate it from one end to the other.

The "Chinese Lot" was like a second schoolyard to us.

We named it because a Chinese family owned a big house adjacent to the lot and ran its family laundry business from there. The owner never complained about us as we actually kept the lot clear of debris. Our parents knew the place well and we all lived within a 5-minute run home. It was perfect. We played punchball in the Chinese Lot, although when the weather got cold, hitting the ball with our bare fist just wasn't practical so we'd play touch football instead. Sometimes we'd play a little rough, resulting in injuries. Once, I was pushed so hard that I fell forward slashing my wrist on a piece of glass on the ground. I had to get some stitches at the hospital and can still see the scar some 60 years later. Speaking of scars, just about every guy in the neighborhood sported some sort of scar, which, like a tattoo, was proudly displayed. We'd compare scars from time to time, boasting about the size, number of stitches we needed and of course, how you got it in the first place. My wrist scar was nothing when compared to the scar on my friend Richie's arm. One day while retrieving a ball, he climbed a five-foot-high chain-link fence. You know, the type of fence with twisted, V-shaped wires at the top – as if the fence was meant to continue up further and was left incomplete. Well, that wire embedded itself in his arm as he began to climb down the other side and ripped an 8-inch tear into his arm, luckily missing an artery. He had to get about 40 stitches and was the talk of the neighborhood for months. Thank God no one ever topped that feat.

Once the winter set in, ball-playing was limited, so we resorted to other sources of amusement. Right after Christmas, the Chinese Lot was used by some of the neighbors to discard their holiday trees. The older guys would pile up the trees and set them on fire at night so the full effect of the fire could be appreciated. The blaze was spectacular. Exciting as it was, we were always nervous about the fire spreading. The older guys seemed to take some precautions, but the sparks from the dried out pine needles still shot into the cold air like a swarm of newly hatched fireflies. While the needles burned up, the trunks of the once decorated Christmas trees would begin to ignite. After a while, the glowing and charred pine trees would burn out leaving a pile of blackened trunks and limbs. Days after the fire was completely out, the real fun began. We would set up an obstacle course where each of us had to jump over the burned up trees. To make it a real challenge, the length of the jump increased as we added more and more trees. The outcome was a bunch of guys covered in charcoal, black from missing the jump and landing atop a tree. The winner, who jumped the farthest, was usually the one with the least charcoal on his clothes, hands and face. Of course, most of us got punished for this when we got home. Promising our parents never to do this again, we all secretly looked forward to the next years' tree-jumping event.

STREET GAMES

In the 1950's, playing outside the house was commonplace. I'm sure the lack of modern conveniences such as air conditioning and, of course, electronic games and computers were some of the reasons we ran out the door to play whenever we could. Besides playing in the empty lots and schoolyards, we often played other games on the streets that are now referred to as "street games". In general, these games did not need a ball to play.

"Ring-A-Levio" was one of the rougher games we played. This was a fast game that had roots going back to the game of Tag. However, in this game, two teams, with an equal number of players would oppose each other. Both teams would essentially be "it" with each team trying to find the opposing players hiding somewhere within a predesignated area of play. Each team had to select a place called "jail" where the tagged players would be held. The object of the game was to be the first to capture all of the opposing team's players.

Tagging is actually a misnomer, as a true capture meant that the player was physically contained with his forward motion stopped. If the game was played on the streets, the teams would usually agree to keep from too much rough housing. However, when roughing was allowed, many an opponent had to be taken down to the ground to be considered captured. Prisoners were freed if they were touched by any player on their team that reached the jail safely. There were many variations and nuances to the game which added to the fun. It was a game that required a high degree of teamwork. Playing against the bigger kids was always a disadvantage but being fast on your feet gave you a fighting chance of winning. Sometimes these games would go on for hours or had to be continued the next day due to darkness or the dinner hour.

"Johnny-on-the-Pony" was another rough team game. The members of one team lined up one behind the other. One guy would lean on a wall or grab hold of a fire hydrant that we called a "Johnny Pump". The other players on the team would bend forward at the waist and hold on to the guy in front of him. Players from the opposing team would jump on their backs one at a time until the weight of all the players brought everyone to the ground. I remember playing this a few times with guys my own size. However, once I experienced the pain of having some bigger kid land on my back, I quickly retired and became a spectator, a much safer role to play. Nevertheless, hearing the moans and groans of the players always amused everyone.

Other games we played were very fast ones but not nearly as rough as Ring-A-Levio or Johnny-On-The-Pony. Much has been written about them, including Tag, Hide-And-Seek, Skelly, Kick The Can, Red Light Green Light, and so on. In the past sixty years, life on the streets of Brooklyn and the other boroughs of New York City has dramatically changed. The sight of seeing kids play at these games is extremely rare and almost non-existent.

During this time, adult supervised sports became more and more prevalent, which in-turn, replaced the need for children to organize their own play called "pick-up games." Development, congestion, and concerns for the safety of the children due to a changing society, led to parents developing many fears related to having their children play unsupervised outside their homes. Gradually, this resulted in the stifling of opportunity to just go outside and play, and more reliance on supervised activities.

    The street games were played less frequently until the knowledge of the games themselves, handed down for decades, became just a memory in many neighborhoods. Articles and books have been written about street games including the history of their demise. The loss of this culture is sad to see especially for those of us who experienced it all when we were young. What is learned in school is a vital part of everyone's development and the success of society. But, the creativity, imagination, and teamwork learned through those street games, while considered play, can't always be learned in school. Boy, how I do miss them.

OUR HORROR HOUSE

Imagine two seventy-year-olds reminiscing about their Horror House adventures when they were boys. Well, it happened when my cousin Jim and I got together at a recent family dinner. Talking about those days with our other cousins brought back so many memories – from the fun we had to the girls we went out with. One of our favorite places to spend some time in the summer was Coney Island. It was only a few miles walk or a short two-stop ride on the train for us. One of the first things we'd do was to go through the scariest ride they had. Monsters popping out, spooky lights, and eerie sounds were some of the effects a rider had to come face to face with.

One of our friends, Michael, had a large, open basement in his home. One day, someone had an idea to start a club and create our own horror house down there. We could push each other around in Michael's father's desk chair. The chair was perfect. It was very large, so we'd sink into the seat and couldn't see anything around or behind us. Now that we had the place and the rolling chair, all we needed was to get the props ready and our horror house was in business. We all pulled together and rummaged up masks, flashlights, and strings that we could use to simulate spider webs. Someone was able to get his hand on a spooky record to play to add to the sense of horror.

With Michael's basement lights shut off, one of us was wheeled around. The others would be doing their best to scare the pants off the rider with their flashlight shining up from their chin so the light would accentuate white snarling teeth. It was kind of scary, but the worst part was the roughhousing that the rider was subjected to. You see, most of the guys just gave up on the theatrics and took turns jumping and pouncing on the rider to scare him. It wasn't too scary – it just hurt a lot. Once, I got a bloody nose from all the pouncing. The guys thought I had brought fake blood but no, it was real. Soon after, the whole idea was dropped and the horror house was closed for good.

DON'T MESS WITH DRACULA

One summer, a new Dracula horror movie came out. It was a must-see movie for my friends and I. So one Saturday afternoon, there we were, about ten guys sitting tightly together in the same row at the movies in Coney Island. The movie went along as expected, as we were no strangers to this genre. As I recall, there's a long segment in the movie where Dracula's crypt is under attack by one of the heroes of the movie. The scene is set at Dracula's castle at the time his crypt is discovered. As Dracula and his undead vampire wives are asleep in their coffins, the sun begins to slowly set. Why in heaven's name would a vampire killer attempt to destroy Dracula just minutes before he will rise beats me, but remember, it's a movie. Within minutes, the hero drives wooden stakes into the hearts of the vampire wives as they lay in their coffins. With this deed completed, he then turns to Dracula's coffin, which was now empty. Again, why wouldn't he first destroy Dracula then move on to the other vampires? I don't know, it's a movie!

Here's where the rubber met the road, the point at which all ten of us screamed unashamed and uncontrollably – all of us holding tightly on to each other. The door to the crypt opened loudly and Dracula suddenly appeared at the top of a stone staircase. With his red piercing eyes bulging, blood seeping down from his mouth,

James C. DeLaura

and fangs protruding, he looked really pissed off. That scene did it for me for quite a long time. The suddenness of Dracula's spectacular entry into the crypt left such a scary impression on me that it lasted the rest of the summer. I simply could not shake loose that horrible image of Dracula's red eyes, bloody mouth, and menacing fangs. Whenever I was alone in my house, I would enter each room with a crucifix held tightly in my hand at arms length as if it were a lantern lighting my way. Falling asleep at night was no fun either, but with my crucifix lying on my chest, I felt better and made it through. None of the guys ever talked about that day at the movies, not wanting to relive the horrible scene but more so that no one found out what wimps we were.

CHAPTER EIGHT

The Ball Games

There were so many games played on those Brooklyn streets, many of them involved playing with some sort of ball. Practically all of the ball games played were based on the game of baseball, truly the national pastime in those days. This was the case whether you hit a ball with a bat (baseball or softball), a broomstick (stickball), your open palm (slapball and boxball), or your closed fist (punchball).

We played every one of these games whenever we could. If there weren't enough guys to play a team game with the full fanfare including running bases, we would resort to using what was called "automatics". Typically, we would play this version of the game in a schoolyard. Automatics meant no running of any bases; instead, we would designate areas and distances where a single, double, triple and home run would be called. Hence, if a ball was safely hit into one of those areas, a corresponding base hit was "automatic." Likewise, boundaries were established to create areas delineating automatic outs. In this way, we could enjoy a game with as little as one opponent. But there were other forms of amusement at our fingertips, most involving very little to no investment at all. If we could get roller skates, we skated. When the skates got old, we'd recycle the wheels and make box scooters.

We'd sit down in clearings inside the empty lots and play with our rubber army soldiers, making dirt roads for our toy jeeps and troop trucks to ride over. The tracks left by their rubber wheels added a level of realism to our war play. I remember lying on the ground so that I was at eye level with those dirt roads, pushing my truck while I pretended to make truck engine sounds. Our imaginations would take us back to medieval days as we made wooden swords and shields for dueling each other as Knights of the Roundtable. Yes, our imaginations played a huge role in our everyday leisure time. Where else could we simulate a house of horrors in a friend's basement, as our club members would go through their initiations?

I believe we were blessed having the opportunities we had. As simple as they were, they are pleasantly engrained in my memory. Hearing a child saying they're bored never sat well with my friends or me. Memories built on our experiences have been for me, more lasting than recounting the score achieved playing some video game.

IT'S ALL ABOUT THE BALL

Having the right ball for the games we played was very important. Due to the nature of the ball games we played, a hollow rubber ball was most popular. However, there was a big difference in the balls available. Other, lower-cost balls were okay for games such as stoopball, box ball and slap ball. However, whenever the game required some degree of pitching proficiency, as in stickball, the harder, more grip-able ball made by the Spalding Company was preferred.

The best ball to use when playing stickball was the "Spalding High-Bounce Ball" made by the Spalding Company. This ball, called a "spaldeen," was definitely the ball to get if you wanted to throw some real mean curves. Ironically, it was so well balanced, it was also a great ball to hit. Towering home runs and wicked line drives were a cinch for the better stickball players in the neighborhood. The downside was, they were often lost on a high rooftop. When neither of these balls was available, we might use an

ordinary tennis ball; however, the resiliency was not as good as the others. It would tend to split in half when hit too hard. The games we played with these balls offered us a variety of techniques and competitive fun every day. I became quite effective at pitching a knuckleball. When I threw it correctly, it looked like a great pitch to hit to the batter and was hard to resist swinging at. But by the time it reached the batter's box, it would suddenly drop so low that it was practically impossible to hit at all. It was my "go-to pitch" when I was ahead of the batter.

Today, my sons and I fondly remember the times we played stickball together in our New Jersey backyard. They were quite young when I introduced them to the game and, like me, seemed to love the competitiveness of the sport. The only pitch they had trouble with was my "knuckler". Boy, they hated that pitch and tried so hard to hit it. Sometimes they actually did, and it was always a home run for them. They would always complain when I threw it, but I just couldn't resist wanting to relive those days playing in my Brooklyn schoolyard.

James C. DeLaura

STOOPBALL

The ultimate game played on the stoop was "Stoopball." This was a very popular game for the kids but so, so annoying to our parents and other adults in the area. You just had to play it when no one was around. Before explaining why it was so annoying, let me describe how the game was played. The only equipment was the ball, and unlike other games we played, any old rubber ball would do. The team, or person, that was "up" had to throw the ball against the stoop, carefully aiming at a point on one of the steps. The object of this maneuver was to hit a point and have the ball sharply bounce back into the street (beyond the sidewalk and curb). Missing the point, the ball would lack any snap and typically be caught easily by the fielder. Once the ball cleared the curb, you would receive a base for every bounce of the ball in the street.

The actual number of bases awarded was equal to the number of bounces made before the fielder caught the ball. If anyone on the fielding team caught the ball on a fly (i.e., before it bounced), an out was declared immediately. The team that was "up" then proceeded to throw the ball

Stories From A Brooklyn Stoop

against the steps until three outs were made and the process repeated.

Of course, both teams meticulously kept the score as some cheating was commonplace. Unless an actual scoreboard was set up, the score had to be constantly stated or someone's lead would slowly melt away. Even then, arguments arose unless a third party scorekeeper was engaged. We'd play 5, 7, or a full 9 innings, boy, what fun! But, let's revisit why the game was so annoying to most adults. First of all, they were nervous wrecks whenever a car came down the block knowing their kids were playing in the street. We would all develop a knack to know when it was safe to play and when to move to the side. Our parents didn't like our knacks to say the least. Then, there was the noise. Picture a ball thrown against the stoop, missing the point and ricocheting backward slamming against an aluminum storm door. It sounded like hitting the door with a sledgehammer. Thinking back, they were so right. But who cared back then? Not us! Just the same, our game was ended sooner or later with the threat of telling our fathers how we misbehaved that day. Sometimes we were spared and our fathers never found out, other times we weren't so lucky, and once again punished by sitting still on the stoop for an hour or so. However, when it came to playing in front of my house, we had the extra-added attraction of my grandfather. My grandfather would typically be relaxing on his set of wooden crates, enjoying his unfiltered cigarettes, directly in earshot of the stoop. As a new grandfather, I can hardly wait to play with my grandsons – being there with my son, Chris, as he teaches his boys to play ball and other games. In the 1950's and 60's, my grandfather had no interest in our games. Many a game of stoopball was suddenly ended when my grandfather lost his patience with us. Sometimes he would just take the ball from us while at other times he'd fling one of his broomsticks at my friends and me as we hurriedly escaped. Thinking back, I can't remember a time when he actually hit us - I guess it was his way of asserting his authority and clearing out the stoop.

Fortunately for us, my grandfather seemed to forget the whole incident the next time we played. If we were lucky enough not to make much noise, we might even be rewarded with a ball that he previously confiscated from us. One day, I remember opening up a small corner cabinet in his apartment and finding a dozen or so rubber balls that he had taken away from us or found on our block. I learned quickly how to butter him up so I could get one of those balls now and then. It was sort of a win-win situation for both of us.

STICKBALL

Stickball was a great game and accounted for countless hours of fun for my friends and I. When we played a one-on-one game, a box was drawn in white chalk against a wall in the schoolyard. This box would represent the strike zone that the pitcher would aim for. Applying the rules of baseball, if the pitched ball hit the inside of the box (including the actual lines of the box), a strike was called. Questionable calls were always decided by examining the ball immediately after the pitch to see if any white chalk had rubbed off on it. To ensure the validity of this method, the pitcher had to wipe off any chalk before he could throw the next pitch.

Swinging at a pitch without hitting it was also a strike and like baseball, a pitch landing outside the box and not swung at was called a ball. Keeping an accurate count of the balls and strikes was usually a source of controversy.

Stories From A Brooklyn Stoop

To overcome this, the actual count had to be repeated often by the two players, almost as if a sportscaster was announcing the count with each pitch. To keep an accurate score, a makeshift scoreboard was drawn on the wall near the play area. Each inning the score would be recorded with the chalk and the game went on.

PUNCHBALL

Punchball was another game where a simple rubber ball was all we needed, yet with so little equipment, we spent many hours testing our skills, competing and building camaraderie. The explanation of the game is in the name. A rubber ball would be tossed up in the air in front of you and just before it reached about eye level, you would strike or punch it with your bare closed fist. Missing the ball with your swing was an out. For the most part, the game was played much like stickball, except that there were no pitchers, no balls or strikes called, and you used your closed fist instead of a bat to hit the ball.

We mostly played in the Chinese Lot, but playing in the street was another option. Of course, there was the added danger of the cars coming down the block. But as with stoopball, we were really savvy about it and tried to stay clear of them. The real danger was damaging someone's car. A broken antenna, scratched door or dent on the hood was a real problem for us. While we rarely caused any damage, most of the nicer cars were usually parked where the owners knew we would not be playing.

Sooner or later, a hit ball would bounce on top of a parked car and catch an adult's attention. After being scolded or threatened, the game had to move down the street. We all thought this was a small price to pay and the game went on!

SLAP BALL

For my friends and me, the best place to play slapball was at the corner of a quiet block with a T intersection. It isn't a very sophisticated game; all you needed was a catch basin grate for home plate, a manhole cover and some chalk for laying out bases. Since cars would usually be parked on one or both sides of the street, they became makeshift bases. Their side view mirrors made great touchpoints for first and third base. Second base was either a manhole cover, if the location was just right, or we would simply draw a square on the street with some chalk. A short distance or line would be agreed to, which meant the ball had to pass the line to be in play. Once the field was defined and the sides chosen up, the game would begin.

A pitcher would use an underhand motion to toss or

pitch the ball towards the hitter. The ball had to bounce once before reaching the hitter who waited with the open palm of his hand ready to "slap it" into the field. Sometimes, variations in pitching techniques were allowed and a slight curve was put on the ball. To be considered a fair ball, it had to bounce in the infield, thus keeping control of the area that the game was played in. This was a great way to play a form of baseball in a relatively small area. Of course, as with all the games we played in the street, we had to watch out for cars coming down the block or the occasional adult "checking" on his car if it happened to be one of our bases. As you might expect, our slapball games had to be fairly mobile if we needed to make a quick getaway.

BOX BASEBALL

When we couldn't play in a schoolyard or park, we might play Box Baseball – a simple game played by two people with a rubber ball and where the field of play was just the sidewalk. Since the concrete sidewalk is poured in squares, the game would be played using three squares in a row. The players would face each other and straddle the two squares on the ends, keeping one square between them.

To play the game, the ball was lobbed (pitched) into the center square (box) with enough oomph to reach the opponent's box on one bounce. The opponent (batter) would slap the ball with his open hand into the pitcher's box. As with stoopball, each bounce would be treated as a base hit. Box Baseball was a quieter game and tended not to irritate any adults in the area. A great game on a Sunday afternoon as the extended family gathered around waiting to start dinner.

BOX BALL

Box Ball was played with just two squares. Each player would straddle his box in the same way they would if playing box baseball. As long as each player was able to hit the ball back into this opponent's box, the game went on. Much like tennis, a point was scored when a player was unable to hit the ball back to his opponent's box. It was a game you could play almost anywhere, as it was fairly quiet except for the players' loud yells typical of a competitive sport. Years later, residing in an active adult community, I was pleasantly surprised to see the game was still alive and well at a neighbor's house. As I visited my neighbor one day, we began to talk about the old days in Brooklyn. He took me out to his garage and showed me the box ball court he had painted on the concrete floor. Even in my sixties, I couldn't resist his challenge to play. He beat me squarely and I got quite a workout.

HIT THE COIN

There were other games played using the countless concrete sidewalks of Brooklyn. Everyone seemed to love playing Hit the Coin. This was a game boys could play against girls or even adults. The only skill required was a sharp eye and steady hand. A coin was placed on the joint between two sidewalk squares. One player stood at the far edge of his square and the other player would stand on the far edge of the adjacent square. The object of the game was to hit the coin with the ball. Typically, the first player to strike the coin with the ball 11 or 21 times would win. Basically, you earned one point each time you hit the coin and two points if you flipped the coin over. If you were lucky, the coin would end up closer to you after it was hit and your opponent would have a harder time hitting it.

I loved playing whenever we visited some of my aunts and uncles or my parent's friends. Hanging around with the adults was not something I looked forward to. If there were no other kids around, my siblings and I would ask my father if we could go outside to play hit the coin. As it was a rather sedate game, we never had a problem getting his permission. In fact, he even supplied the coin.

Years later, I introduced the game to my own boys. The competitive nature in each of us was evident as we all tried hard to hit that coin. Even though I towered over my young sons, their nimble fingers and lowness to the ground made them very good players, often beating me fair and square. That game, learned on the sidewalks in Brooklyn, was an instant hit with them.

CHAPTER NINE

Rules of the Game

Over time, we decided there needed to be some structure added to our games. The terms and expressions we used were sometimes handed down or created due to an obvious need. In reality, they became rules that usually everyone abided by. Doing so also prevented the tough guys from making up their own rules as a game went on. Well, at least most of the time.

CHIPS ON THE BALL

This was a common expression used before a game began. It was very important for the person supplying the ball to invoke this before the game began. It was basically a form of insurance and, as we all know, you can't take out insurance after one incurs the loss. It simply meant that the owner of the ball would be given a new ball or reimbursed for the cost of the ball by any player that lost it. Typically, this would happen when a batter hit a ball onto the roof of a nearby house or building and couldn't retrieve it. The system seemed to work, unless some older kid gave you his middle finger instead of a new ball.

Money being as tight as it was for all of us back then, most of us would try almost anything to retrieve the lost ball rather than have to buy a new one. For example, if a ball was lost down a storm sewer which was fairly common when playing slap ball, or punchball, we would resort to the "wire hook" to try to retrieve it. This device was made from a simple wire hanger that we would find in our parent's clothes closets. Untwisting the hook end and then straightening the wire out we would shape the other end into a rounded loop, slightly smaller than the diameter of the ball. Bending this loop about 90 degrees to the straight wire we would lower into the sewer through the large opening at the curb's edge. With a lot of practice, we became quite good at hooking the ball onto the wire loop. Carefully pulling up the wire we got our ball back. It was a bit of a messy operation, but well worth the trouble. Sometimes we would even be fortunate enough to find another ball in the process.

HINDOO

Hindoo was an expression that seemed to be only recognized if playing under poor conditions, or if some sort

of hazard presented along the playing field itself. This expression actually had its roots from the term "hinder" but as with many words and terms used in the neighborhood, it became another Brooklynism called "hindoo". If play was interfered by a pile of leaves, some foreign object, or a number of other obstacles, hindoo could be called and a "do-over" would be allowed.

The merit of such a call might be debated, but a final decision was usually made very quickly. The downside of calling a questionable Hindoo was an invitation to the opposing team to look for any way they, too, could do something over. Nevertheless, it was there to be used by either team. I remember making a Hindoo call when someone's younger brother wandered onto the field at the same time I dropped a ball that was hit towards me. The kid didn't really interfere and the error was entirely my fault. As you would expect, I lost the call but it was worth the try.

FIRST DIBS

Calling First Dibs meant that a player or entire team was laying claim to using the playing field as soon as it became available. Let's say a couple of players showed up at the neighborhood schoolyard and wanted to use the stickball area. If others were already using the area, they would shout out, "we have first dibs," to those playing. By doing so, any other players showing up before the game was finished would have to wait until the first dibs guys played at least one game. Of course, when this happened, the game had to move briskly along or the team waiting would become restless, usually resulting in some argument or fight. As with the Chips on the Ball expression, calling First Dibs only worked when others respected the convention. The bigger kids would simply take over the field if they wanted to.

SUCK THE FIELD

One might think this is a hard expression to explain, but it just meant that, before a player could get up to bat, he would have to play at least one inning in the field. The only exception, of course, was when your team was first at-bat at the start of a game. This was not an expression you had to invoke at the start of a game as it was basically understood that it always applied. I believe it came about to eliminate a team putting in a ringer at a key point in the game. Back then, the designated hitter concept wasn't used in professional baseball, so we had no example to follow.

THE COIN TOSS

Not many coin tosses were used, probably because very few of us had any money on us. Using the matching finger method was common, but the gutsy approach was with the use of the bat. We developed an interesting way to choose sides or determine which team got up to bat first and who had to take the field. One team captain would take hold of the bat with a one-hand grip. Then, the opposing team captain took hold so that his hand would touch his opponents, but further up toward the bat handle. This would be repeated until there wasn't enough bat left to grab. Once this happened, the captain not holding the bat was allowed one kick of the bat to try to knock it loose from his opponent's grip. If the bat wasn't knocked loose, the team captain holding it chose his first player or selected whether he wanted to bat first. Far from Robert's Rules of Order, but it was fun and it worked!

CHAPTER TEN

Boy, How We Played

There were actually no limits to our imagination. In those days, we didn't have anywhere near the resources or means to buy things as we do today. Electronic games and toys were almost unheard of. The one toy that stands out in my mind was a battery-powered robot I received for Christmas one year. The advent of home computers was decades away and an electric pinball machine was as close to modern-day electronics as one could get.

Summertime meant no school and the best time for kids. It was the most productive time for us to invent new games or to use the materials at our disposal to create our own fields of adventure.

THE GAME OF BRISK

On some days, we'd spend hours sitting in front of a house without a stoop. The front of the house usually would have a clear space to the right or left of the front door. Adults would sit on their folding chairs when they got home from work. During the day, the area was all ours.

We would sit in a circle and play one of our favorite games called Brisk. This is an Italian card game, actually called "Briscola." The game was played using a 40-card deck. Before play could begin, all the eights, nines and tens would be removed from a standard deck of playing cards. While the game could be played with two to six players, we would typically play a game with two or four players.

Much has been written about how to play Briscola, but the basics of the game were handed down by adults and some of the older kids in the neighborhood.

    The game was so popular, we'd spend countless hours in the summer months playing it. The hours went by as we sipped soda and munched on a generous supply of sunflower seeds – much the same as what you see professional baseball players eat when in their dugout. We would spit out sunflower husks, making mounds of the stuff surrounded by glops of sticky soda residue on those concrete sidewalks. Cleaning up this mess was a must if you wanted to play in the same area again, a small price to pay for an afternoon of fun.

PLAYING THE PART

I loved playing stickball, especially with my friend, Mike. We would always start with each of us naming the major league baseball team that we'd pretend to be for the game. My favorite choice was the New York Yankees. However, it wasn't always that way. Rooting for the Brooklyn Dodgers seemed like the natural thing to do for a kid from Brooklyn. Knowing everything about the players, collecting their baseball cards and staying abreast of the team's standing in their League was all part of being a loyal fan. A rare trip to Ebbets Field with my father was a huge treat for me. Once, a groundskeeper handed me a ball that fell out of bounds. When I got home, I wanted to tell all my friends that I caught it but just couldn't. Imagine how much mileage I would have gotten with a tale like that! In any event, I was ecstatic and never forgot that day.

Like many Brooklynites, when the Dodgers moved to California in 1957, I dropped them like a hotcake. This was a rather devastating time for my friends and me, but we got through it. Soon after, without another National League team in New York, we gravitated to rooting for the

Yankees. Whatever hang-ups we had making this change were quickly erased as we embraced our enchantment with Mickey Mantle. It wasn't really hard for ten-year-olds to become fans of a new team, and Number 7 sure made it easy for us. He became an instant hero with most of us. The Yankees became, and still are, my favorite team.

In addition to knowing just about everything there was to know about the Yankees, we also kept up with some of the other teams, especially when we liked a particular player. Of course, collecting and trading baseball cards made it that much more fun for us. Just before Mike and I would play, we would flip a coin or use the two-finger method to choose which team we would be. Since we both wanted to be the Yankees, it was a bit of a competition from the outset. As we knew so much about the former Brooklyn Dodgers, they frequently ended up selected as the opposing team. Now came the fun as we would announce the name of the player we were while at-bat. We would then bat right or left-handed depending on the player. Thinking back, I believe we actually thought we were that player at-bat. Many times, when I was at bat as Mickey Mantle, I'd feel the extra power in my arms as I swung for the fences. You know, sometimes it would work. Talk about a vivid imagination!

EN GARDE

Having an almost endless supply of wood, crates, and bushels on hand at my grandparent's house was a creative child's dream. My cousins, friends and I became somewhat proficient for our age with the use of basic tools like a hammer, handsaw, file, and screwdriver. Using these tools, we would craft our swords using a wooden slat from an empty apple crate. A slightly rounded tip would be shaped and a crossguard would be nailed on the sword in an attempt to protect our hand. A shield would be made from the cover of a bushel as it had a natural curve to it. We would tie a rope across the inside of the cover to hold onto. Then, it was en garde!

Dueling with wooden swords was fun but could easily end up with the combatants cut up and bruised. The crossguards that we attached to the wooden swords were far from foolproof and resulted in many a cut hand. Winter gloves were later introduced to soften the blow, but once ruined by the repeated pounding we got into trouble with our parents for that. It was a risk we all had to take as no one dared back out of a good sword fight. We would be Knights of the Roundtable, Roman Gladiators, or bands of Pirates as we fought those make-believe battles in hand-to-hand combat style. The goal of our games was typically to outlast all of the opponents. We had to come up with a way to determine when someone was mortally wounded. To keep it simple, we would take turns judging each contest. If a dueler struck a mortal blow to his opponent, he would shout out, "You're dead." We had to rely on everyone's honesty in this regard, but the judges would have the final say and it generally worked out. Again, we were always diligent in keeping watch for any adult that could see us or it might be another punishment back to the stoop, or something worse.

HAVE SKATES WILL TRAVEL

An activity that many baby boomers can relate has to be roller-skating. Besides the bicycle, skating through the streets was a common method of getting around town. During the weekend, the roller-skating rink was not only a great place to have fun, but, as we got older, it was a surefire way to meet girls. By the time you were interested in meeting them, you'd better be a proficient skater. Looking like a clumsy ox on skates was not good. Making sharp turns, stopping on a dime and some speed skating ability were all the attributes you needed. Getting any fancier, like figure skating would be a no-no amongst the guys back then.

Once a pair of roller skates was fairly worn out, they were recycled. We incorporated them into a homemade "box scooter." This contraption was made of four simple parts, plus some nails or screws, all usually readily available. For my cousins and me, it was a snap as we had our uncle's inventory of discarded fruit boxes on hand. The actual parts included the following:

- One 3 to 4-foot long piece of 2" x 4" lumber (commonly called a two by four)
- One wooden apple box
- Two short pieces of 1" x 2" lumber (called a one by two)
- One roller skate

The skate was separated into two sections by unscrewing the plate that held the front and back wheels. Each piece supported one set of wheels and was secured to each end of the underside of the two by four. The apple box was secured to the front end on top of the two by four and the one by two pieces secured on top of the box for handles. And there you had it – a box scooter. Once all the parts were assembled, we would decorate the scooter with bottle caps and banners if we had them. Since the apple box had one open side, we could use it to store things we might need to take with us, or carry groceries from a store we were sent to. My cousin and I once made a two-man box scooter. I think it was the only one in the neighborhood and it sure looked great. It went pretty fast as we would both push it, much like riding one of today's skateboards. The problem with it was its poor turning ability. After several near-miss accidents and with much disdain, we dismantled it. Whether using our box scooters to get around the neighborhood or racing down our block, it beat walking most of the time.

Stories From A Brooklyn Stoop

James C. DeLaura

WANNA FLIP ME?

Collecting baseball cards back in the 1950's was much different from modern-day collecting. Once I'd save up some money, I'd buy a pack of baseball cards. The first thing I did was to open the wrapper and pop the flat piece of bubble gum from the pack right into my mouth. While working that piece of gum into a chewable wad, I'd anxiously look through the pack for my favorite players. I'd always carry my cigar box with me and place the cards in them, keeping the "good" ones separate from the others. Once I had a sizable collection, I was ready to "flip" them against someone else. The goal, of course, was to win as many cards from an opponent as possible. It all started by approaching someone saying, "Wanna flip me?" This slang expression was uttered just about every day during the summer. Guys would roam about the neighborhood searching for someone to risk their baseball cards against. You had to be pretty good at it to keep growing your collection.

There were many versions of flipping cards, with the most common one being the "side flip." You would hold a card lightly on its long side using your thumb on top and your index and middle fingers on the bottom. With a flipping motion, you would gently toss the card in the air while releasing your grip. At this point, the card would flip side over side until it lay to rest on the sidewalk. A card would end up with the picture up (called heads) or with the picture down (tails). The number of cards being flipped had to be agreed on before anyone began flipping. Hence, I would say something like, "I'll flip you five," which meant, I'll flip five cards and you had to match my flip exactly to win. I usually had good control so I tried to get all heads or all tails. If I accomplished that, once my opponent failed to match mine, I would win and collect his cards. It made for good drama if you flipped a lot of cards, say ten, and got all heads or all tails. Your opponent had all the pressure as one slight extra jerk before his release could cause the card to end up on the wrong side and the match would be over. Holding each card in the same position and releasing it the same way each time was a challenge and usually separated the frequent winners from the frequent losers. While all of this was going on, you had to pay attention to the card you were flipping so that you didn't risk your favorite cards in the match.

Another version was called "closest to the wall." In this game, once deciding how many cards would be played, you would crouch down on a line about eight to ten feet from a wall and fling your card with a flick of the wrist towards the wall. Each player would take his turn flinging one card, then the other would go until all cards were played. The card closest to the wall would win and you would take all the cards played in the match. Once in a while you would get a "leaner," which, unless knocked down by an opponent's card, would be considered the closest to the wall.

One of my favorite versions was "topsies." Each player would take turns placing his card flat against the wall and then release it. The card would flip side over side until it settled on the sidewalk. Placing each card in different positions along the wall before releasing it would result in cards lying down in a rather wide area. The only rule was to stay within the bounds of the game, say about four feet wide along the wall. The player topping (touching) any one of the cards would win all the cards played up to that point. In this game, the longer it took to top a card, the more cards would be played and be at risk. The more experienced players would always know when it was the right time to top a card and end the game as the winner.

Hours were spent playing the game. Sometimes, when a group of us gathered to flip cards, we would also use the opportunity to trade with each other. Unlike some collectors, with their sealed box sets and leather-bound albums, our cards were often dog-eared from the constant handling and flipping. We would even attach some of the cards to our bikes using an ordinary clothespin. The card was placed so it would touch the wheel spokes as we rode the bike, making that distinct clatter sound. Boy, it sounded like we had a motor driving our bike. Somehow, many of us lost track of our baseball cards as we got older. Years later, as young adults, my friends and I would share stories about the valuable cards we had, like Mickey Mantle and Roger Maris. Of course, at the time we were collecting these cards, I, like many others, didn't think much about their future value. By the time we did, it was too late, as we couldn't find them no matter how much we rummaged through our old closets. We always seemed to blame our mothers and fathers for the loss, thinking they threw out our cigar and shoeboxes as they cleaned out their closets and basements. What a shame!

When my sons, Chris and Matt, began collecting and trading baseball cards, they were much more meticulous and kept their cards in albums and plastic sleeves. Neither of the boys or their friends ever "flipped" cards and I always thought that was a lost boyhood tradition. But still, they seemed to get tremendous joy collecting them and visiting trade shows with me. As adults, they haven't had to blame their parents for losing their cards and hopefully will one day benefit from the value they might bring. My son Matt had a knack of finding uncommon cards of high value. He did so with his baseball as well as his basketball card collections and always exhibited pride in his acquisitions. While my memories of my baseball card collecting will always be special to me, my eldest son, Chris, often warmly reminisces about the time he and I built his 1985 baseball card set from scratch. We weeded through many a pack of cards and display tables at trading shows to finish the collection. On his own, Chris maintained a master list of the cards he needed to complete that set. He carried the list everywhere he went where there was an opportunity to trade or buy the needed cards. That set, he says, will always mean a lot to him, a set he made with his Dad.

TAKING THE CITY OUT OF THE BOY

There's an expression I've heard that states something like "You can take the boy out of the city, but you can't take the city out of the boy". When I was in my early teens, I loved spending time in the "country" as it was referred to. My Aunt Rita and Uncle Sam's home in Long Island was the place to be. I'd have a great time playing with my cousins. The setting was very different from my neighborhood back home but playing in their backyard or the nearby wooded area was always a fun-filled adventure. I enjoyed playing catch, going hiking, or spending time on some common hobbies my cousins and I shared.

My aunt and uncle were super nice and made me feel special. Of course my cousin and I would get into some sort of trouble now and then, but there was no stoop in front of their house to do penance on. Just a brief reprimand and off we went. I always had a great time there and looked forward to my next summer visit. Nevertheless, returning home after my week long stay, I couldn't wait until I got back to the streets of my Brooklyn neighborhood. Back to my friends, and the stoopball, stickball, and punchball games we played.

CHAPTER ELEVEN

Discovering Girls

Teenage years began with a slow transition from having fun with the guys to a more serious direction where school and social interaction became increasingly important to me. Summertime was the absolute best time to meet girls. Between the beach, parties, or just hanging out, there was always an opportunity before you. The real favorite past time was not baseball for most guys – it was the girls. For some, their experiences started in their early teens. Most of my friends and I were what they call, "late bloomers," as we were usually preoccupied with sports. By the time we reached 14 years old, we finally bloomed.

PRESSURE FROM EVERYONE

Once my interests turned to relationships with girls, pressure from parents seemed to have taken a new direction. Instead of just asking me to be on time for supper, they typically wanted to know where I was going, with whom and what time I'd be home. Things loosened up with time as I tried not to abuse any of the privileges I had.

Nevertheless, the "when we were your age stories" were leveled at me often. It's funny how, as annoying this seemed to me back then, I used the same tactic with my two boys as they were growing up.

As a young teenager, I took part in my Church's Confraternity of Christian Doctrine (CCD) Program. At that time, boys and girls that attended public schools were able to attend a religious education class once a week, held on Wednesdays. If you attended the class, you were allowed to go to the dance held in the Church basement on the following Friday night. We referred to this dance as Confraternity, and it was usually well attended. I recall the dance being chaperoned by some of the parish nuns. Besides keeping the noise levels under control, they were very good at keeping dance partners separated by at least a couple of inches. They would usually poke the boy with their finger if he got too close to his dance partner. If you respected the rule, they didn't seem to mind slow dance couples to dance cheek to cheek. In those days, the girls would tease their hair into huge mounds and keep it firm with tons of hairspray. With my face somewhat buried in this beehive, as they were called, the scent of their hairspray lingered long after the dance was over. Even today, when I smell hairspray, I can easily drift back to those 1960's dances, this time without the poking by the nuns.

FIRST LOVE

My first real heartthrob was Jane, a pretty girl about my age, whom I had met through a mutual friend. We seemed to immediately like each other, and the mutual attraction was obvious. Soon after meeting, we "went out," which in those days meant we were officially girlfriend and boyfriend. Going to Coney Island with Jane was special. We would enjoy the beach or take in a movie or some of the rides. One of our favorite rides was a house of horrors. The ride was sort of a tunnel of love with scary effects. It was a lot more fun riding with Jane than with the guys as I did years before.

We'd ride in one of the large cars that looked like a king's throne winding in total darkness as the many scary faces and props popped out at us. Of course, we were oblivious to it all as our eyes were closed and our lips pressed up against each other most of the time. It must be love I thought, but it only lasted through the summer, then it was on to other things, particularly school. After Jane, girlfriends seemed to come and go; I suppose it was all part of the growing up experience. Never any hard feelings, each party would just move on to the next love of our very young lives.

SPIN THE BOTTLE

I was invited to my first real boy-girl party when I started my first year at Junior High School. By then I thought I was a seasoned teenager, having just gone out with Jane. I also soon discovered that an advantage of going to Junior High was meeting a new crop of girls. The opportunities to socialize were abundant and parties and other get-togethers seem to pop up every month or so. Hearing about the games that were played at some of these parties, such as Spin The Bottle, I was looking forward to my first party. As Halloween approached, I was invited to a costume party.

While I wouldn't dare tell a soul, with the help of my mother, I assembled my costume using my white slacks, my father's Navy blouse (shirt), bow and sailor's cap. My

Stories From A Brooklyn Stoop

mother said I looked very cute in my sailor's suit and I remember hoping the girls at the party would feel that way too. Being considered "cute" was a real compliment back then. Well, the costume was a success and they all made a fuss over me. It was great. The party was given by one of the girls at the school named Diana. After her parents greeted us, they left the apartment, leaving us unchaperoned. This was new to me, but I welcomed the free atmosphere at the party. Soon after, Diana took out an empty soda bottle and announced, "Time for spin the bottle." As there were more girls than boys at the party, I knew this would be a very interesting night. Diana led off explaining how the game was played and gave the bottle a spin. She seemed to know what she was doing as the bottle came to rest pointing to a guy she seemed to like. They kissed and some of the girls giggled. Soon after, another girl gave the bottle a spin, which pointed towards me, and we kissed as well. This went on for some time with my good luck holding out, as I seemed to be kissed pretty often. After a while, everyone enjoyed some junk food Diana's parents had prepared and danced to 45's that played on her turntable. It was a great party, everyone

Stories From A Brooklyn Stoop

said, as the parents returned and the party ended. I especially enjoyed the gathering, even though my lips were really sore, but what a way to go, I thought.

FASHION STATEMENT NO-NO

In the 1960's, thirteen-year-old boys did not care about making their own fashion statement. However, when they discovered girls, they would suddenly pay attention to such things. I was no exception as I began to look for the right "look" to make a splash with the girls. Muscle shirts or motorcycle jackets weren't for me. Maybe the fact that I had no muscles to speak of, or a motorcycle to ride on, contributed to that, I'll never know. White clinging t-shirts with a pack of cigarettes rolled neatly under one sleeve didn't do it for me as I neither smoked nor would spend a penny to buy a pack of cigarettes. Then, all of a sudden, poncho shirts came into style, and just about every cent I had was spent on building my wardrobe of poncho shirts. The classic feature of these shirts was the matching v-shaped front and back. The shirts were worn outside your trousers to truly appreciate them. I had three of these shirts in bright solid colors, including orange, green, and blue. They were typically worn with my white pants so they would be even more noticeable. Finishing off my outfit was a pair of socks that matched the color of the poncho shirt I was wearing. The pants had to be just the right length to reveal the colored matching socks. Boy, did I stand out. What the heck was I thinking? Walking through my neighborhood, I thought I looked really sharp. By the time the summer faded away and school began, the fad wore off for me. I never did wear the ponchos outside of my pants and was happy when my teenage body outgrew them.

JIMMY TECH

For high school teenagers, expressing their team spirit was second nature. Attending your school's events or rooting for them at competitions was all part of the experience. I for one, loved to wear my high school sweater whenever I could. One spring day, I decided to wear my Tech Sweater in the neighborhood. It was a white woolen sweater with thin blue stripes on the upper part of the sleeve and a large letter "T" over one breast. It was rather neat I thought, and I was proud to wear it outside of the school. As I was only one of a handful of boys attending Brooklyn Tech High School from the neighborhood, the large letter T stood out. Most of the sweaters and jackets were worn by students going to Lincoln High School, the local school in the area.

Brooklyn Tech was located in downtown Brooklyn and most people knew about its rigorous standards and its reputation for turning out would-be engineers. Sometimes, it was a good thing for me as it was very impressive to some of the girls, but at other times, wearing it could get me into a little trouble. The Lincoln jocks might not be so impressed, especially as our schools competed fiercely in football. Nevertheless, I was still a neighborhood kid and that always held more weight than the school you attended. Soon after I began wearing the sweater, some of the girls nicknamed me, "Jimmy Tech." I remember often passing a group of them hearing, in unison, "Hello, Jimmy Tech." That was rather nice, I thought, as that sweater got me noticed.

OUT OF MY LEAGUE

At fifteen years old, I think every guy has probably

had a crush on some older girl, whether they'd admit it or not. When it was my turn, I became infatuated with an older girl on my block. Anna was a beautiful, dark-haired woman in her mid-twenties. She had a great smile and always spent a little time with me, saying hello or asking how school was going. I know she liked me, but only as a young boy, the son of one of her neighbors. Nevertheless, I enjoyed the fact that Anna didn't talk down to me and seemed genuinely interested in what was going on in my life. When the weather was nice, I would do some schoolwork on our stoop, waiting for her to emerge from her front door. One day, she pulled up with some guy in a very nice car. *Get real*, I thought to myself, and just like that, this one-sided relationship finally came to an end. In many ways, I was glad this happened, for I found myself comparing girls my own age to Anna. Since that day, I considered her a friend and soon developed a comfortable relationship with her. From time to time, we had light conversations about my school or goings-on in the neighborhood. While it was back to reality for me, it would be a couple of years before I actually got over the older woman, a feeling that I'm sure was shared by many teenage boys.

DUEL AT THE LANES

I had a teenage crush on Jenny and planned to ask her out. I soon found out that she was dating a guy named Paul, a kid that moved into the neighborhood a couple of years prior. While this was obviously a major stumbling block for me, I didn't give up on the possibility of dating her. I looked for any opportunity to talk to her and it was obvious to Paul. As a result, he and I never got along and there were noticeable bad vibes between us. Neither of us made any effort to make things better. We frequently bowled at the neighborhood bowling alley and would see each other there from time to time. Sometimes Jenny was there with him and I would always say hello to her, which I knew annoyed him.

Growing up with the movies of the day, a duel, with swords or a pistol, was one way to win over a damsel or defend one's honor when it was compromised. So, I thought to challenge Paul to a "Duel At The Lanes." Well, I didn't actually say a duel, and there was never any intention of using a sword, just my bowling ball. At that time, it was common to bowl against someone for some small wager, say one or two dollars. The match was set up by challenging the opponent to anywhere from one to three games, stating the wager in advance. By adding the word "stuck," such as, stuck and a dollar meant the loser had to pay off the wager, but was also "stuck" or obligated to pay for the winner's cost of the game.

Paul accepted my challenge and we agreed the wager would be stuck and two dollars for each of three games. On the day of the match, I was very nervous as I wanted so much to impress Jenny. Placing this extra pressure on myself, I asked my friend Jimmy to come with me for support. Paul, on the other hand seemed rather calm and relaxed with Jenny in his corner. I felt as though I had already lost the match as I could hear Jenny cheering him when it was his turn to bowl. In my corner was Jimmy Shongod - absolutely no match for Jenny!

Whenever I approached the lane for my turn, I was all tensed up, and as they say in the sports world, "choked." I couldn't control my nervousness and was off my usual game from the onset. My scores suffered and Paul beat me soundly all three games. He was gracious about the whole thing as I handed him the money I lost in the wager. It was hard for me to face Jenny, but she was as nice as Paul as she waved goodbye. Afterward, Paul and I were much more friendly towards each other. Soon after, I forgot about Jenny and went on to my next Brooklyn girlfriend. I also practiced bowling a lot more.

LOVE FOUND ON THE STOOP

At 15 years old I met Joanne, a neighborhood girl who lived three blocks away. I liked her as soon as we met. Looking for a reason to pass her house, I would walk the family dog down her block in the hopes she would be outside. One day, she was there, sitting on her stoop, so I struck up a conversation with her. Her mother was also there and was very much into the conversation, as she knew my parents. I didn't sense any interest from Joanne, so we just remained casual friends. From time to time I would see her, but nothing came of it. Later that year I learned that her family had moved to a new place in Bensonhurst, which was a few miles away. Once in a while, Joanne's name would come up since my sister, Lilly, and her boyfriend, Larry, were close friends with Joanne's brother and his girlfriend. Through this small grapevine,

Joanne and I would exchange polite hellos.

Much to my surprise, when her parents gave her a sweet sixteen party, I was invited. While having mixed feelings about it, I ultimately decided to go to the party. I didn't know any of Joanne's friends and soon learned that she was dating some guy in a band. After a while, I realized coming to the party was not a good move on my part and left early. I later wondered why she invited me in the first place and it would be years later that I learned it was her mother's idea. Determined to put this behind me, I decided to forget about Joanne and moved on.

About a year later in May of 1964, my sister got married and I was one of the ushers in the bridal party. Joanne's brother was also an usher, so the limousine taking me to the church stopped at their house to pick him up. As the limousine pulled up, I looked out the window and saw Joanne sitting on her stoop. Although she was not invited to the wedding, she was dressed up to attend the church ceremony. She sat there, with her hair done up, and looking downright beautiful. I think right then and there I was struck by the so-called "thunderbolt" as I stepped out of the limousine. I was decked out myself, feeling quite

confident in my black tuxedo as I approached her. We had a short conversation and I asked if we could talk again after the church ceremony. She agreed, and when we met, I asked her to a dance being held the following Friday night. Joanne came with me to that dance and then to my high school prom the following month. Little did I know then that we were just beginning our life long journey together.

CHAPTER TWELVE

More Short Stories

I'm amazed by how many stories I am able to recall from my years in Brooklyn. Bringing them to life in this book may bring back some of the stories of your own past or perhaps just bring a smile to your face. Some of them have been downright silly and others reflect the simple and carefree nature of my experiences growing up in Brooklyn. Sharing them through this book has been such a tremendous joy.

DOES YOUR DOG BITE?

Not all memories of my childhood in Brooklyn were happy, funny, or memorable ones. Some, I'd like to have forgotten, but something always seems to rekindle the thought of them in my memory. There's a classic scene in a movie where the main character is standing at a corner waiting for a walk sign to flash and finds himself next to a man with a dog at his side. He asks the man if his dog bites, for which the man replies, "No." Proceeding to pet the dog, he is nipped on his finger and confronts the man saying, you said your dog doesn't bite. The man turns to him and says, "Yes, but that's not my dog."

It makes a good case showing why you should not assume things. It also reminds me of a very unpleasant time in my early life when I assumed a dog was friendly, went to pet it and was severely bitten on my face. Unfortunately, stray dogs were a common sight in the 1950's, and seeing one of them with dog tags was rare. Once I was bitten, the dog ran off and was never found. As a precautionary measure, I had to go through a full course of injections for rabies treatment at the hospital. My recollection of the incident is very vague as I was relatively young, but my memory of the treatment has remained somewhat clear. Once a day, for fifteen days, my father would take me to the hospital to get an injection in my stomach. It was awful, and I have this image of standing in front of my father as he held my arms at my side. The doctor lifted up my shirt and injected me with a needle in my stomach and I would scream with pain. While it was one of the most unpleasant experiences of my life, I remember the warm and comforting feeling I had when my father held me in his arms and said, "Don't worry son, everything will get better."

PIZZA BOY PLOY

My friend, Ricky, learned how to make a pizza pie before he knew how to throw a baseball. His family owned a local pizzeria/restaurant and he learned how to make a great pie at a very young age. One day, a group of about four of us decided to take a long walk to Sheepshead Bay. Along the way, as we winded through the town, we passed a pizzeria – so we stopped and looked inside through the store's large picture window. A young pizza maker was flouring a mound of pizza dough on the stone counter as he prepared to make his next pie. Ricky gestured for the guy to toss the stretched out dough in the air. The guy just smiled and shook his head from side to side as if to say no to this kid outside his window. We all went into the store and Ricky seemed to challenge the guy, saying he could toss that dough up in the air, why doesn't he?

As it turned out, the guy was the owner's son and must have found the whole thing quite amusing as this 13-year-old kid taunted him. Much to our surprise, he made us a bet. If Ricky could toss the dough into the air and make a good pizza pie, he'd give it to us for free. If not, we had to pay for it and eat it anyway. Ricky smiled and accepted the challenge. He was given an apron, washed up, and before you knew it, there was a mound of dough in front of him. With the precision of a seasoned pizza maker, Ricky began pounding the dough and sprinkling flour on it now and then. Next, he began opening the dough with his closed fists, placing it back on the counter, adding more flour, stretching and slapping the dough. Then came the moment of truth as Ricky slowly spun the limp mass with his closed fists before tossing it several feet into the air in front of him. The owner's son watched in amazement as Ricky caught the stretched out dough and placed it on the waiting pizza paddle called the "peel." With the dough on the peel, Ricky stretched it out again then stirred in the sauce, added the cheese and then some oil and spices.

The guy then took over and placed the pie into the oven. We all knew Ricky could do it, but the young pizza maker was noticeably amazed. He was so impressed that we not only got the pie for free, but he gave us the soda as well. Of course, we had to come clean as to how a 13-year-old could make a pie like that. It was all good, in fact the owner came out of the kitchen and said he knew of Ricky's

Stories From A Brooklyn Stoop

parent's restaurant. These pizza makers knew they were snookered but didn't seem to mind.

JENNA'S NIGHTMARE

Moving from grammar school to junior high ushered in a transition period for me. Thinking about the future became more important than playing with the guys. I got serious about my schoolwork and became a fairly good student. By my second year, I had passed a special admissions test to attend Brooklyn Tech High School and suddenly found myself actually on a path to my future career. I wanted to become an Engineer for quite some time and seemed to be off on the right foot. However, I also felt there was nothing wrong with having fun along the way. The summer before entering high school was kicked off with a bunch of graduation parties for many of the girls in the neighborhood.

It was June of 1960, and it seemed as though we were going to graduation parties every weekend. Jenna, a sweet girl in the neighborhood, invited my friends and me to her party. As we arrived, we were greeted by her father, a rather large man with a distinct Italian accent. I remember feeling a little uncomfortable as he looked each of us over with his piercing eyes. Boys in our neighborhood quickly learned that fathers are very protective of their daughters, especially Italian ones. We were directed down to the finished basement and, as typical, all of the boys huddled in one area of the room as the party got underway. Within minutes, one of the guys pointed out a homemade bar and moved to check it out. There were no bottles in the bar or on the wall rack behind it. We assumed Jenna's father had taken them away in readiness of the party. After eating some hot dogs and pizza, one of the guys comes running down the steps to the basement. He had just used the bathroom on the main floor and discovered the mother lode of booze in the bathtub. He was so excited that we had to calm him down. It wasn't long after that we heard a big commotion coming from the main floor of the house. It was Jenna's father yelling and screaming. I remember hearing him shout, with a broken English accent, "Somina Bitch!" By the time we all went upstairs to see what was going on, it was clear that all the guys were being thrown out of the house. *Bummer*, we all thought as we hurriedly marched out the door while poor Jenna stood helpless with tears running down her face. My buddy, Jimmy, and I can still see Jenna's father's red face as he threw every boy out.

Once away from the house, we found out that two of the guys concocted a plan to smuggle out a couple of the liquor bottles from the bathroom. Standing inside the bathtub, one of them opened the window while the other positioned himself in the driveway. The noise they made must have been so loud that Jenna's father suspected something was going on and caught them red-handed. We never understood why Jenna's father would put his liquor supply in the bathtub, but at that point it really didn't matter. We all suffered for the actions of the two knuckleheads that tried to take the liquor bottles that day. In some way, we were okay with it, as we had our hot dogs and pizza and still had each other.

WINO FISHERMEN

Living in the southern part of Brooklyn, my friends and I were fairly close to places like Coney Island and Sheepshead Bay. Both locations offered us opportunities to do some fishing without having to rent a boat. The Coney Island Pier and bulkheads in Sheepshead Bay were our favorite fishing spots. One winter evening, we decided to head out to the bay to do some night fishing. Ritchie, a big hulk of a guy who was about three years older than the rest of us, offered to take us there in his car. We had a special bond with "Tiny," as we nicknamed him, and would occasionally hang out together. Getting permission from my father was no problem even though it was to be a late night. So with friends Jimmy, Anthony, and Ritchie, there we were in Sheepshead Bay doing some whiting fishing.

Within minutes of throwing in our lines, Ritchie pulled out a bottle of some red wine to warm us up. Without hesitation, we passed it around, each of us taking a short swig. As luck would have it, just as I took a taste, my father's car pulled up into a spot about 50 feet from us. Crap, I shouted as I struggled to shove the cork back in the bottle. I tossed the bottle into some nearby weeds as a sense of panic ran through me. Calming down was a challenge, as he would surely know we were up to no good. Like most parents, my father could usually tell when I was up to something. Then I began to worry about him smelling the wine on our breath as we spoke with him. Once my father reached us, he said he was out on an errand

and decided to see how we were doing. We all tried to act natural and seem happy to see him. It was hard to talk while trying not to come face to face with him, but apparently it worked.

Once my father went home, we searched high and low in near darkness but couldn't find the bottle. I caught some flack from my friends; actually, they were really pissed off. We caught a lot of fish that night and our adrenaline kept us warm. Days later, Jimmy, Anthony and I all agreed that it was a good thing I lost the bottle since it tasted horrible. Hot chocolate would have been much better.

PIERRE THE FRENCH POODLE

My friend, Anthony, would babysit for his sister's adult friends now and then. One Friday night, Jimmy and I stopped up to see him on our way to the bowling alley. After a while, Anthony told us to go see the French Poodle named Pierre, lying on a bed in one of the rooms. When I entered the room and called his name, the dog moved its legs to reveal his underside. I didn't think much of this, probably just a nervous reaction to me entering the room.

Then, Jimmy went in after me and came back to join us. I asked him if Pierre did anything when he was in there. He looked at me with a smirk and said, "No, what are you talking about?" When I explained, both Jimmy and Anthony laughed and said I was crazy. Then, both of them entered the room to see Pierre's reaction, but there was none. As soon as I joined them, Pierre, who was lying on his side, opened his legs to again show me the jewels so to speak.

It was hilarious and we kept testing the theory that Pierre had a thing for me by taking turns going in and out of the room. Each time I came in, the poodle would react the same way – we couldn't stop laughing. Of course, I was the brunt of the laughter for quite a long time. My only retort to them was, I guess I just have that animal magnetism everyone talks about!

BEACH BLANKET COURTROOM

It was just some clean fun on Manhattan Beach, but no one bothered to read the posted rules and regulations. There was always a group of guys and girls meeting at the

James C. DeLaura

beach, doing what young teenagers did in 1960 - have fun. That day, one of the guys suggested we toss girls up in the air as they sat on a beach blanket. The girls were not forced to participate; in fact, they would be disappointed if they didn't get their turn. It was two or three tosses and on to the next girl. While no one ever got hurt, I suppose if one of the guys lost his grip, there could have been a fall. But falling on the sand didn't pose a problem for us and it wasn't given a second thought.

Suddenly, as if out of thin air, two men approached the group and shouted at us to stop what we were doing. They flashed badges and identified themselves as the police. Crap, everyone seemed to say as we dropped the blanket to the sand. We stood like sheep, huddled in silence around the two cops. We never knew what hit us as they had us gather our things, then marched us up to a nearby Parks Department building where the walkway met the beach. The girls were free to go, they only wanted us. Once inside, we were asked to show identification. Our names were written down and they gave us a stern lecture on why engaging in rowdy activities on the beach was not permitted. Each of us was handed a summons to appear in

Court to answer for the violation. Most of us were worried that our parents would find out about this brush with the law. Some of us speculated whether this would go on our "record" even though we didn't know what that actually meant. Later we decided not to say a word about this to our parents and hoped for the best.

When the day came for our appearance, we all met and went together to the downtown Brooklyn Courthouse. Suddenly, my name was called and, as I walked up to the bench, I wondered why I had to be the first one. The Judge had the offense read aloud and he directed me to describe what I did. I nervously answered that I threw girls up in the air as they sat on a blanket on Manhattan Beach.

The Judge evidently had a sense of humor as he asked me in a startled way, "And you did this by yourself?" At that point, I felt a sense of relief as I further explained that I was one of six guys that did the tossing. He brought the rest of the guys up to the bench, gave us a two-minute spiel on being more responsible and fined us each two dollars. At this point, we all felt relieved and knew the fine was more symbolic than punitive. We never tossed the girls up in the air on the beach again and our "record" remained spotless. Better yet, our parents never found out.

REVENGE OF THE MOLARS

I believe most people would agree that going to the dentist is not at the top of their hit parade. Unless you were suffering from a toothache and expected some instant relief from your visit, you would probably prefer to do something else with your time. As a young teenager, I would most definitely agree with that premise. So, wouldn't you think every dentist would go out of his or her way to make a patient's office visit experience as pleasant as could be? You would think so, but when I was a young teen, one of the most disturbing images imbedded in my brain is that of a picture that was openly displayed at my dentist's office. The framed picture was mounted on the wall directly in front of the dentist's chair so the patient would come face to face with it at every visit. While I tried to look away, I couldn't stop staring at it during my entire time in the chair. As I recall, the detail was intricate, showing a hill with a hangman's gallows planted at the top. Against a sky thick with gray clouds, a pair of dental pliers was hanging from the gallows. All along the way up the hill and surrounding the gallows were hundreds of molars all seemingly cheering the event on. This was a big contrast to the type of wall art you find in a dentist's office these days. I often wondered why my dentist would have such a picture in his office. Ever since then, the mere thought of having a tooth extracted conjures up thoughts of that gloomy image.

CHAPTER THIRTEEN

Learn While You Earn

By the time I was in my early teens, my need for money took on a higher level of importance. I could no longer hope for small change from my parents for good deeds, so I kept my eyes and ears open for other opportunities. Along the way, I learned a lot about people from the shops and streets of Brooklyn.

BACK ROOM BAKER

One of my first part-time jobs was working in a local Italian bakery. Walking only a few blocks to the store was great, as I didn't waste any time traveling. While I had hoped for a position serving customers or making cakes and donuts, I was assigned to the back of the kitchen where I would clean out all the vats, pots and machinery they used to make the dough. I had to scrape out as much of the leftover dough as possible, and then scrub the equipment with a hand brush. This would take hours to do and was repeated day after day. My hands were not only clean as a whistle but they had a puffiness to them from the constant attack of the leftover yeast, dough and water.

You know that great aroma coming from a bakery? That distinct smell of fresh breads, cakes, and pastries! Well, it didn't exist at my workstation where the pots, pans and machinery were located. After about two months on the job, I decided to quit as my hands became softer and silkier than my mother's. Looking back, the only thing I regretted leaving was the free donuts I'd get whenever I worked there.

BAG POLICE

A friend of mine put me in touch with the manager of a local Mom and Pop type supermarket. It was not as large as the chain stores of the day but it was successful in the neighborhood it served. One drawback, however, was that I had to take a bus to get to the store.

I thought I'd be assigned to someone who would teach me the ropes; maybe working as a stock boy, or perhaps working up to a cashier. I couldn't wait to start. Much to my disappointment, I was asked to check bags and carts that customers would typically take with them into the store. The owner didn't want anyone walking around his store with an open bag or personal shopping cart. So there I was, standing just inside the door surrounded by bags and carts that I had taken from the customers for safekeeping. My job was essentially to take the customers' bag or cart and place a clothespin on it with a card that had a preprinted number on it. I then gave the customer a card with the same number on it so they could retrieve their bag or cart when they left the store. Simple? Yes, but it was an extremely boring job. Imagine standing for hours at a time guarding bags! I often stood daydreaming, asking myself why I left my bakery job. To amuse myself, I would conjure up a scenario in my mind where I'd mix up the numbers just to see what would happen when the customer returned to retrieve their bag or cart. But I never acted on any of these ideas; after all, I was in charge of the bags - I was the Bag Police.

After a few weeks at this, I asked the manager if I could do something else in the store. Apparently, there were no applicants on a waiting list to become a bag monitor, so I was stuck. I even cited my experience with my uncle's fruit and vegetable business, but to no avail. About a week later, I told him I needed to leave the job to devote more time to my studies, but I would stay on until he got a replacement. Of course, my story was not entirely the case, but I was trying to be diplomatic. As it turned out, I ended up policing the bags another three weeks until he found my replacement. I never understood why I offered to stay on, but felt it was the right thing to do.

THE SODA JERK

Soon after leaving my supermarket job, I was hired to work in one of the neighborhood luncheonettes. My job was to serve customers frequenting the luncheonette for a fountain soda or quick bite to eat. While I did some light cooking of things like burgers and fries, I was basically a "soda jerk," a term that came about because of the pulling, or "jerking," motion used while operating the handles at the soda fountain. I hated the name, but at the same time, I loved the job. It put money in my pocket; more than I earned from any of the jobs I had before it. It was yet another great way to meet girls and I enjoyed the interaction with the customers.

I had never aspired to work at the luncheonette because it was always well manned by the owners who were in their thirties. They never used any of the neighborhood kids to

Stories From A Brooklyn Stoop

work there and handled all the work themselves. That was okay by my friends and me because the owners were a great bunch. We all enjoyed being there for a soda, light lunch or some dessert. To date, the mere thought of their homemade rice pudding brings back thoughts of a delicious time in my life. They were fun to be around and they told the greatest stories. Sometimes we'd go there just to listen to an afternoon baseball game and be amused by their colorful commentary.

When they decided to sell the luncheonette, we were all sad, to say the least. We could hardly wait to find out who the new owner was and how they would run the place. Within a few weeks, we realized things would be different at the luncheonette. The new owner was an older man, with what seemed to be, a serious demeanor. We all knew that the carefree times there were gone forever. Our fears became reality the very first time he abruptly asked a group of other teens to leave. Evidently, they had lingered in their booth after they finished their sodas and Sol, the new owner, wouldn't have it.

As time passed, Sol hired and fired several of the neighborhood teenagers at his luncheonette. Seeing an opportunity, my friends Jimmy, Anthony and I applied for jobs. We were all hired to work during different shifts throughout our school week and on weekends. Sol assigned me to work behind the counter, which was much to my liking. We learned our job responsibilities quickly, but we also learned that Sol was a serious businessman and was quite good at making money. He changed the menu, set new prices and watched how every cent was spent on supplies. He closely watched us, especially when other kids came into the luncheonette. We assumed he thought we would give them freebies when he was preoccupied. Of course, he was right, so to keep our jobs we didn't do it. Once he gained confidence in us, from time to time he would leave the luncheonette in our care to go on local errands. We all respected the trust he had in us and never took advantage of him.

After a while, I became quite good at making any egg dish a customer wanted and on occasions even got a tip for my efforts. I would sometimes hear someone complimenting Sol about me. However, I was disappointed that I never received any positive feedback from Sol directly. I felt he didn't want me to get a swelled head, so to speak, and ask for a raise. He was a decent boss, but a cheap one at that. Besides making all kinds of egg dishes, I was proud of my fountain drinks. One favorite drink of many Brooklynites was the Egg Cream. There weren't any eggs or cream in the drink so I never understood how it got its name, but it sure tasted good. The chocolate egg cream was made at the fountain. I'd first put chocolate syrup in a glass, add some milk, and top it off with seltzer stirring vigorously as I filled the glass. The creamy head slightly overfilling the glass and chocolaty body really looked great. One day a customer was so impressed with the egg cream I made for him that he told Sol, "This kid makes a great egg cream." As I overheard him, I felt rather proud of myself and hoped that Sol would acknowledge it. When the man left, Sol walked over to me and said, "You're putting too much milk in the egg cream." Well, so much for an acknowledgment! Consequently, I had to cut back on the milk, but the drink wound up tasting more like a fizzy chocolate soda than an egg cream. Somehow, I found a way to make my kind of egg cream without Sol noticing. All the while hoping no one paid me a compliment in front of him, or worse, to him directly.

Looking back, I believe working at the luncheonette gave me an appreciation of the notion that the customer came first.

NOT SO SPEEDY MESSENGER

It was my senior year in high school and my friend Perry got me a part-time job at a messenger/delivery service he worked for called, "Speedy Messengers." While only paying minimum wage, it was enough to cover the cost of my leisure activities. It was an easy job and didn't seem to interfere with school. The owner was quite a character and seemed to treat us all like numbers. The office was rather crude with absolutely no attention paid to the decor or the employee's comfort. Describing it as "plain vanilla" would be a compliment. The area where we waited for our assignments was small and stuffy with the smell of body odor and stale cigarettes filling the air. Many of the people working there as messengers were rather uncouth looking. Perry and I never worked together but we compared notes all the time and laughed about all of the crazy goings-on there.

I only worked about two or three hours a day, so my

time there was just bearable. Most of the time on the job was spent on a pick-up or a delivery and not in the office. Besides, I had only planned on staying on until graduation in June, just a couple of months away. After working there about a month, I was given a large envelope to deliver to 36th Street and assumed it was a Manhattan address as all my deliveries up until then had been there. After leaving the subway in Manhattan, I took out the invoice and realized that the delivery was for an address in Brooklyn. Panic set in as I raced back to the subway. By the time I had gotten back to Brooklyn, I was already over an hour late. Finally, I made the delivery and hoped no one called the office to check on it. The entire time I kept worrying how this would play out with my boss, after all, we were "Speedy Messengers."

So there I was racing back to the office when I saw a phone booth in the subway station, so I called my boss. I decided to hide my mistake by concocting a cover story. I told him that after I made the delivery I had to go to my school to take care of some pre-graduation matter. When I said I would be late getting back to the office, he didn't utter a sound, then said to get back as soon as possible. As

I hurried through the subway station, I tripped and fell down about four or five concrete steps. As you would expect, I really got hurt, tearing my pants and cutting up my leg and knee. As I lay on the floor for a moment in pain and bleeding, I knew I was really in trouble. Hobbling to catch a train, I decided to go home and later called the office again. As I started to tell the boss my tale of woe, he stopped me cold and said, "Don't bother to come back, you're fired."

The events of that day taught me several lessons. First, don't assume things without checking the facts. Second, don't lie as it will only catch up with you somehow, someway. And lastly, don't work for another messenger service ever again.

THE NEWSSTAND

During my first year at City College, I worked at a newsstand located inside my local subway station. The station was on the elevated portion of the subway along what was referred to as the "F Train." Due to my schedule, I was able to work three hours a day, four days a week before I traveled up to 138th Street for class. My first chore was to haul several heavy stacks of bound-up newspapers up two flights of steps to the newsstand. Once I brought up the newspapers, I'd get the stand ready for the morning's sales. In addition to the newspapers, I'd sell all the typical newsstand items like cigarettes, cigars, gum, and candy. The owner's stand did a brisk business every morning. I had to learn the prices and make change quickly, especially for the customers running from the token booth to catch their train.

It would get extremely hectic for ten minutes or so, then there'd be a lull, followed by another frenzied charge at the newsstand. Some of the commuters were in such a hurry that they never had time to buy anything but the newspaper. They would just drop their money, take the paper and run. On rare occasions, a customer would grab a paper and yell out, "Catch you tomorrow," which meant they would pay me the next day - which they always did. While some of them ran like hell to catch their train, others seemed to like stopping by the newsstand for a pack of gum or a snack before they got on the train. Some of them bought the same things every morning, like this one guy who bought these tiny cigars in a flip-top box. I always had them ready for him with a pack of matches, which he

Stories From A Brooklyn Stoop

seemed to appreciate. After a while, he'd plunk down his money and say, "Keep the change." With this success, I tried my best to have items ready as other regular customers stopped by the stand. I think some of them bought the item, whether they needed it or not, as they liked the attention I would give them. Once in a while, I'd get a smile or a wink from a customer. I always liked that.

One thing about that stand that impressed me was how it was put together. My father was a good friend of the owner and actually built the stand from scratch for him. With only an eighth grade education, my father was about the handiest guy I knew. There was no way anyone could figure out how to get in this fortress of newspapers, gum and cigarettes. It was like a pyramid with a secret entrance. When I left for the day, I would leave the proceeds (less my tips of course) in a plain brown paper bag in a special place for my boss to find. One of the best compliments I received was when he told my father that his proceeds were hardly ever above $100 a day until I took over the job from the previous guy. My paper bag usually had between $110 and $130 a day. I never speculated as to why, but I knew that the owner did. While I don't recall what I was actually paid for this job, I'm sure it was fair. Anyway, it fit in nicely with my schedule that year and was another great experience for me in dealing with people.

THE WEDDING CATERER

Once my school schedule changed, I had to leave the early morning newsstand job. After a couple of months, I went to work at a catering hall where wedding receptions, engagement and anniversary parties were held. Again, my father helped me get a job as a waiter through his friend, Sal. I gladly took the opportunity, even though it meant working on Saturday and sometimes Sunday. It paid very well for the time and the $18 a day plus any tips I might get went a long way.

I was 17-years-old, but I vividly remember my first day at the catering hall. My father told me to bring a white shirt, black pants and bowtie and ask for Sal once I arrived. Finding Sal was pretty easy; he looked exactly as my father described, a good-looking guy in his forties with jet-black wavy hair and a continental swagger – very suave. He greeted me warmly, said nice things about my father, and introduced me to everyone. He led me through the ornately decorated facility and showed me the layout for the tables needed for that evening's reception. He then handed me off to a waiter named Richie, a rather salty mouthed guy in his thirties. Richie showed me how to set up the tables, from the lace tablecloths and setups to the last ashtray.

The captain of the waiters walked around the hall with the table layout Sal showed me earlier. He would move about the room, placing a number placard on each table then shouting out how many chairs should be placed there. The chairs were already resting on top of the table from the previous reception, as it was the practice to enable cleaning the floors. Waiters following him then placed the chairs as ordered. Another set of waiters followed with the appropriate size and color tablecloths. It was amazing how efficient everything went. That day, there were two wedding receptions and a bowling dinner scheduled. I was assigned to the first-floor wedding for about 150 people. About eight waiters, a captain, and my new friend, Sal, the headwaiter, were to provide the service that evening. I recall being a little nervous as I got dressed in the new black and gold waiter's jacket they gave me. I followed the directions given to me and managed to get through the evening without a hitch. After working a few more receptions, I was considered a regular and worked every Saturday and some Sundays as well. As I got to know Sal a lot better, it was clear to me why he was so good at his job. As Headwaiter, Sal would be in direct contact with the bride and groom as well as other wedding principals. He had a way with them all, always acting suavely when in their presence. Sal's famous line was, "What's your pleasure?" as he would gently raise his open hand in an offer of his service. His outgoing persona was exactly what the wedding party wanted; he was no stiff.

After a while, it was clear to me that for all its efficiencies, the place was run in a rather informal manner. The two cooks, Willie and Pedro, were real unsavory characters. They had their job down pat but used more four-letter words than anyone I ever knew. The ovens were located just behind the cook's prep area and the heat was extreme. Instead of sipping cool water, they both drank straight whiskey from a glass strategically placed near their counter. They both downed their drinks now and then. Someone always seemed ready to refill their glasses without having to be asked. Besides chewing out the waiters for getting in their way, each of them would mostly talk about sex.

Everyone was super friendly and seemed to enjoy their job, often joking around with each other. Sometimes the older guys played jokes on each other, even during the reception. I remember one time a couple of waiters knew some of the wedding guests and put them up to playing a trick on another waiter called JP. It seemed that JP hated the sight, smell and feel of anchovies, called "alici" in Italian (in slang it sounds like "al leech"). One of these guests was given some anchovies on a small dish and then called JP over, gesturing as if he was giving him a tip. Then, with the pranksters watching from the nearby kitchen's swinging doors, the guest placed a few alici in JP's waiting open hand. The whole table erupted in laughter as he stood frozen looking at his handful of anchovies, eyes wide with fear and disgust. I was told that the guys watching couldn't stop talking about it for weeks.

As well as things were going for me, there was this one time early on in my new job when I thought I'd be fired. It was a fancy wedding where the waiters wearing white gloves served the meal. This was a tremendous challenge for me as the plates felt unusually slippery in my gloved hands. One of the first dishes served from carts on the banquet floor was manicotti (pronounced "man-i-got"). These delicacies are pasta sleeves about 4 inches long and 1 inch in diameter, filled with a mixture of finely chopped spinach, herbs, and ricotta. This dish is served covered with tomato sauce.

One of the more experienced waiters would place two manicotti onto a dinner plate using a large spoon and fork method they called, "French Service." A second waiter would pour the tomato sauce over them and hand the plates to the servers. The serving waiters would hold as many plates as they could and serve them to the seated guests. You were expected to hold at least two and sometimes, three plates at a time. One thing I later learned was to check for dripping sauce on the sides and bottoms of the plates as everyone was working so fast.

Since I didn't know this at the time, I proceeded to serve the manicotti without checking for drippings. The tables were very long as I recall, seating seven or eight people on each side. The banquet chairs were jammed

James C. DeLaura

close together to accommodate all the guests at the wedding. I literally squeezed my body between two tables, twisting my way through a maze of ladies' fur jackets hung on the backs of their chairs. As I finished serving the last guest in that row, I looked back and saw the remnants of red sauce on everyone's fur jacket.

I freaked out and decided to squeeze my way back down the row discretely wiping off the sauce as I passed by. It seemed to work, but when I returned to the serving cart to pick up my next set of plates, I was covered with the red sauce and my white gloves were unrecognizable. I darted back into the kitchen where I was greeted by one of the cooks who simply shook his head side to side at the sight of me. No words were spoken as I washed off the red sauce from my shirt and changed my gloves so I could get back to my "white glove" serving.

Most people of the time took it for granted that waiters at a wedding reception were already getting a fifteen percent tip off the top of the bill. As a result, tipping during the reception was very rare. Actually, the waiters only received a paycheck for working the reception and the tip was considered a service charge by management, which they kept for themselves.

Under the tutelage of some of the waiters, and, of course, Sal, I quickly learned how to make the guests feel special without being obnoxious and soon found earning tips wasn't impossible. Since the guests at a wedding would be there for five or six hours, the waiter had an opportunity to make an impression on them. On the other hand, he could also be fairly invisible to them, just doing his job without any contact. Learning the ropes from the best, I preferred to become part of the guests' experience. No one had to ask for anything at the table, as I was always one step ahead of them. If I had a really friendly group, I might light cigarettes for the women at the table or offer to bring a guest special drinks that they had during the cocktail hour. There was always at least one guy at the table making a collection for "the kid." I worked hard to do a good job and make Sal proud of me.

For the most part, working at a wedding reception was easy for me, and gave me a great introduction to management at an early age. When I was 19-years-old, my boss promoted me to waiter captain, running smaller receptions, such as anniversary parties or bowling award dinners. About a year later, I became the youngest headwaiter they ever had. I'd direct the receptions in the larger second-floor banquet room. The venue there typically held 200 to 300 guests. I particularly enjoyed wearing a tuxedo and caring for the bride and groom. Directing them through all the ceremonies, such as their grand entrance, first dance, and cake ceremony was fun for me. Salary and tips increased and turned out to be a great way to earn money during my college years.

After the reception was over and the tables cleared off, it was time to settle up. If there were any tips to split, that was the time to do it. Sometimes, the paychecks were given out as well. There seemed to be two distinct groups of waiters. One was what I called the 9 to 5 group. They would leave the catering hall the minute the tips and checks were distributed. The other group needed some downtime to unwind from the evening's work and they were ready to party themselves.

Usually, about ten guys would be hanging around the office and outside sitting area. Most had a drink in their hands waiting for one of the bosses to emerge from the office. A lot of shoptalk amongst the group was common. Smaller groups started to leave in favor of carrying on at a local bar, while others went to a nearby diner that was open 24 hours. Of course, I would be with Sal and ended up at the diner most of the time. Every so often, instead of going out, the guys would start playing craps. It was something to see this game take shape; it was just like in the movies. Watching the game and the characters playing it was yet another education for me. The bets were not large ones, but guys could easily lose $50 or so in an hour. I never understood why they would work about ten hours only to risk what they earned and more to gamble. One day I realized the job was a way of life to most of them. They liked the action of it all and you could see the camaraderie they had.

  During the years that followed, I tried to emulate some of the teachings of my tutor, Sal, but I could never pull off his, "What's your pleasure?" line. Still, the opportunity to learn and develop people skills was ever-present as I worked in this business. Upon my graduation from college, I started my first full-time engineering job. As I left the catering business, it occurred to me that I received two educations that would serve me well in this life of ours.

CHAPTER FOURTEEN

Brooklyn Street Smarts

Some define "Street Smarts" as the ability to manage themselves in dangerous situations, typically in an urban setting or big city. It can also mean just having the right instincts to know how to act in everyday life situations. In many ways, being raised in Brooklyn was like going to the University of Street Smarts. I believe many situations in my life could have had a disastrous outcome if it not for my Brooklyn born senses. Often, I found that these senses helped me make quick decisions and choices that worked very well for me. Sometimes, the outcome was a pleasant or quite humorous one, while at other times, I was simply happy to get out of a situation safely. Yet at other times, you could have all the street smarts in the world and what's really needed is just a little lucky charm.

MY LUCKY CHARM

It was my first time going solo in my father's car and I was so excited. I picked up my girlfriend, Joanne, and was heading out to meet some friends. She was excited, too, as we chatted on the way. Even though I was paying attention to the road, I made a left turn where a small sign indicated no left turns at certain times. It didn't register, and within seconds I was pulled over by a New York City policeman who was strategically positioned on the side of the street. I felt that draining feeling through my body as I was sure I'd be getting a traffic ticket. Somehow, I also knew my father would find out about it and I'd be in a heap of trouble. In the process, I'd probably lose my privileges with his car for a while. Once the cop approached me and asked for my license and registration, Joanne sprang into action. Without any prompting from me, she pleaded my case with the officer. "Please don't give him a ticket, his father will kill him," she said. He just moved back a little and looked over my credentials. Much to my surprise, I only received a warning and avoided the ticket. Any Brooklyn Street Smarts I had couldn't compete with Joanne's beautiful sweet face and persuasive voice that day. She was my lucky charm.

THE BEST DEFENSE

There's an expression that states, "Sometimes, the best defense is a good offense." Hopefully, one never finds themselves in a position to test this when in a dangerous situation. Unfortunately for me, I found myself in such a situation when in my late teens, and my Brooklyn Street Smarts came to my rescue.

It was a spring-like day in May 1966 when my father asked me to take a small load of construction debris to the dumps located a few miles from our house. After I unloaded the car, I was making my way back to the main road towards home. The two-lane roadway was lightly used and meandered through a commercial area before joining a service road parallel to the Belt Parkway. As I was driving, another car pulled up alongside, and then passed me. Once the car was in front of me, the driver began to weave from one lane to another. Since there was quite a distance to travel on that winding road, I looked for an opportunity to move safely around him. With every maneuver, he cut me off, again and again. Even as I slowed to a stop, he would do the same, sometimes coming dangerously close to my car in the process. I decided to just lay back and avoid any conflict. When I finally got on the service road he reappeared, looked directly at me and laughed. I grimaced and turned left, heading home. He went straight ahead and I thought I was done with him. I soon found myself at a major intersection where I had to stop at the traffic light that had just turned red. When I looked into my rearview mirror I saw this guy racing towards me before stopping his car just behind mine. He jumped out of his car and headed towards the driver's side of my car.

With this, I instinctively reached over and locked the doors. This maniac was yanking on my door handle, swearing and yelling at me to get out. He was a rather stocky man, about 40 years old, and was able to rock my father's car from side to side rather easily. As all this was unfolding, I recalled some advice I received years ago to never get out of a car with someone standing there as they could slam the door on you. Seconds later, he released the handle and was coming around to the passenger side. I reached down and found a club my father kept under the seat and grabbed hold of it. I then opened the passenger window enough so his head could fit through. As I suspected, he shoved his head in, probably thinking he could get his hands through as well. But as soon as his head came through I grabbed his shirt and pulled him through the partially opened window. He was startled as I put the wooden club to his temple. My whole life seemed to be flashing before me. All I could think about was how I'd screw up my life if this plays out badly. He begged me to let him go and I shouted something back, which I believe made him think I'd actually would smash him in the head. I took a leap of faith and released him. Like a slimy fish caught on a hook, once released he retreated back to where he came. I was safe again, rid of this guy with a big chip on his shoulder. To this day, while I feel very fortunate that I didn't have to strike him, I wonder what he would have done if I didn't defend myself. Street smarts didn't put that club in my hands, but it sure guided me why not to use it.

SOMEONE'S UP TO NO GOOD

In the late seventies, while on vacation with my wife and young son in Pennsylvania, I had to pull out all the stops to avoid a very perilous situation. On Sunday, the night before we were to head back to our Brooklyn home, we encountered a lone motorcycle rider who proved to be up to no good. At first, it was just a single headlight in my rearview mirror as I drove back to our motel. We had just finished dinner at a local restaurant. At a red traffic light, the biker came up alongside of our car, looked at my wife sitting next to me, then at our son in his car seat in the back. While an uneasy feeling ran through my body, he passed us, crossed my car and quickly turned right and seemed to go on his way.

After driving a couple of miles, I looked in the mirror and noticed that one headlight once again. The roads were dimly lit and, as it was a Sunday evening, not many cars were on them. I had a sixth sense feeling that something wasn't right and felt my old Brooklyn Street Smarts acting up again. Driving a little further, I began to get concerned that, if this was the same biker, I didn't want him to surprise us in the motel parking lot. I ran several scenarios in my head and decided to tell my wife what I was thinking. She was naturally frightened and I hated sharing my concern with her, but I had to at that point. There were no cell phones back then to call the police and my options were dwindling with every mile that we got closer to our motel.

I told my wife I was going to turn into the next strip mall we saw. Once there, I'd park the car and pretend to get out just to see if this guy was actually following us, as I feared. If he kept going, then I was wrong and, oh so relieved. But if not, well, we'll just have to wait and see. Since all the shops on the route were closed, I was hoping my plan would work. Sure enough, the biker shut his headlight off, slowed down and turned into the street adjacent to the strip mall. He just sat there with the motor running. All the while, I pretended not to notice him. Then in a split second, I turned the car around and drove off in the direction we just came from. As I got back onto the road, I could see him turn his motorcycle around in great haste to pursue me.

My thoughts at that point were only on the safety of my family as it was clear to me that he was up to no good. I raced through the streets hitting dangerous speeds, slowing down to run through red lights with horns blaring as I did. *Where are the cops when you need them?* I thought. Finally, after several unnerving miles, I saw a light on at an open motel. I quickly stopped near the office and brought the family in. The manager called the State Police and within minutes a State Trooper was at the motel. The Trooper assured us we would be safe and asked us to get back on the road and slowly drive back to our motel as he thought we would encounter the biker looking for us. He was correct and we could see the guy trolling down the road looking side to side as he passed us. I signaled to the Trooper that this was the guy and he gave chase. We never saw either one of them again.

We went on to our motel and I parked the car away from all the rooms. While I thought I took every precaution to be safe, my wife was still very upset and was completely spent from the ordeal. She was still reeling from the incident and had me barricade the door. As for our son, I'm sure it was like a joy ride as he went right to sleep. Nothing more was spoken about it that night. I said a prayer, thanking the Lord for his protection. I also put in a good word for Brooklyn as I know the street smarts I learned there guided me as well.

SUBWAY SAMARITAN

I'm sure most people have had the opportunity to act on someone's behalf in a moment of need. Certainly, emergency professionals, police, firefighters, and members of the armed forces are examples of those that deal with life and death situations every day. They are trained to act, whether it is on behalf of a total stranger or comrade.

If one is faced with a situation involving harassment, bullying or assault, the decision to act on someone's behalf can be a life-changing event for them. We find ourselves at a crossroad, do we act or do we walk away? Most of the time there isn't much time to analyze the situation too deeply, one's instinct comes into play and the choice is made. We all read the headlines about some good Samaritan being hurt, or worse, as they came to some stranger's aid. We also hear about the heroic action of a good Samaritan, which ended up saving the day. Having that sense of the street is like your personal GPS, helping you navigate through the ordeal facing you.

One spring day, I had to leave my office at about 1:00 in the afternoon for my home in Brooklyn. Taking the subway at off-peak hours was not something I was used to doing. Once the train passed the Manhattan stations, they carried very few passengers to the other boroughs they served. My subway car was empty except for a middle-aged woman sitting alone at the opposite end of the car. I didn't think much of it at the time and continued reading the newspaper I had taken with me. As the train stopped at one of the usual stations, I looked up and noticed that a shirtless man in his thirties stepped in and stood holding a pole at the back of the car. It was strange that he was bare-chested with his shirt tied around his waist as it wasn't hot outside. As the train left the station, he began to swing around the pole while holding on with one hand. Again, I wasn't alarmed but thought he might be drunk or just another kook riding aimlessly on the train.

Within minutes, he walked over to where the woman sat and began to swing around a pole only a few feet from her. In an instant, you could see the fear in the woman's face as she slid down the seat away from the man. He followed her, repeating his swinging act at the next pole near her. At this time, I knew I had to do something. I got up and looked through the cars to see if there was a cop or conductor nearby. Not seeing anyone, I focused on the man who was now in the center of the car. Feeling that I had some time, I sized him up looking for any weapon or object he could turn into one. Once satisfied, I approached him, looked him squarely in his eyes and in my best Brooklyn street language, told him to stop bothering the

Stories From A Brooklyn Stoop

woman.

As I stood between him and the now shaking lady, he stared back at me then sat down next to her. While I was anticipating that this situation might get worse, I asked the woman to move down further and I sat between the two of them. She turned to me and gave me her silent thank you.

Little did I know, but I was soon to become one of this guy's newly found friends. As we sat there almost shoulder to shoulder, I was preparing myself for a further confrontation. Suddenly, as he reached for his back pocket, I got up and took a defensive stance in front of him. Much to my relief, he pulled out his wallet. What now, I thought, is he going to show us family photos? No, he took out some dollar bills and began counting them. With this, I sat down again and told him he shouldn't do that in the subway as he might get robbed. Turning to me, he said I was a good guy, tapped me lightly on my knee, and left the train at the next stop. At this, the woman was noticeably quite relieved. She thanked me again and again. I told her that I would hope someone would do the same if it were my wife or mother in that situation. We were both spared that day. I often thought it could have developed into a more serious situation but felt my approach was the right one for all of us.

FLOWERS FOR EVERYONE

What I've called Brooklyn Street Smarts didn't only apply to a dangerous situation. During the months leading up to my wedding, I had discussed providing flowers for the church ceremony with Father Frank. The good Father said there would be an earlier wedding that afternoon and there was no need to spend extra money on flowers for the pews and aisles. He said the usual practice was to leave the flowers at the church after the ceremony so my fiancé and I took his advice and opted against flowers for the church.

On the day of the wedding, everything seemed to be going well. It was a beautiful day in September and my ushers and I walked the few blocks to the church, catching some rays of sun along the way. Once inside the church, I felt an incredible drain of energy from my head to my toes. There wasn't a flower to be found at the pews or on the altar! I was in a state of panic, took a deep breath and pulled my ushers together to come up with a solution. All I got was shrugged shoulders and blank stares. One of them said, "So, what's the difference?" as I grew even weaker thinking what my soon-to-be wife and future mother-in-law would say to me. Then, I saw flower baskets outside by one of the shrines. I quickly found Father Frank and asked if I could use the flowers for the church ceremony. He said they were leftover from a funeral service earlier that day and didn't see anything wrong with that. When I heard him say a funeral service I got that sinking feeling all over again. Considering how my new wife would feel, I rounded up my ushers and with reverence to the decedent's flowers, took them inside the church. At one point, I actually had to stop one of my ushers from taking the flower basket bearing the "Rest in Peace" ribbon. After all was said and done, it all worked out for the best. *My "Brooklyn Street Smarts" served me well,* I thought to myself. My new wife and mother-in-law even commented on how nice the flowers looked in the church.

WHO SAID NICE GUYS FINISH LAST?

It was our first New Year's Eve and my wife, Joanne, and I thought it would be fun to spend it in New York City.

We had no intention of doing the Times Square scene, for us it was a night out on the town then an overnight stay at a local hotel.

After checking in at the hotel, we arrived at a popular place on the east side of Manhattan at about 10:00 PM. The place was hopping with excitement as it was just a couple of hours before the ball dropped ushering in 1971. At first, we were disappointed that there wasn't an open table or a stool at the bar to be found. Once we worked our way up to the bar, I ordered drinks for us and hoped a stool would become available. After ordering, a guy sitting to the left of me offered his stool for Joanne to sit on. *Boy, that was great,* I thought and accepted the offer. We both thanked him as he drifted into the crowd with his drink in hand.

I noticed a short while later he had worked his way back to the bar about ten feet away from us. I asked the bartender to give the guy a drink on me – it was the Brooklyn smart thing to do. That turned out to be the turning point of the evening for us. In a little while, the guy came over to me and shook my hand saying he never expected someone in New York would buy him a drink for being nice. His name was Bill and he had a distinct southern accent. We got to talking and found out that he was up from the South to temporarily work for the telephone company due to a major strike underway in the City. We also learned he was dating the bar owner's daughter, who was working at the bar that night. From that point on, our money was of no use there. Apparently, he was so impressed by my action that he arranged it with the bar to be his guest and we were treated to dinner, drinks, and New Year's champagne. Bill was later joined by his girlfriend and sat with us from midnight on. Needless to say, we had a ball. I don't recall when we left the bar, but we ate, drank, danced and had an overall fun time with our new-found friends.

TWENTY-DOLLAR BILL

Sometimes, having street smarts means you can tell when you're being conned or mislead. That sixth sense is like a set of antennae warning you all the time. The situation doesn't have to be a dangerous one. It could be a casual incident requiring a simple, yet decisive action. I have a humorous recollection of an incident that happened years ago as an out of town business colleague of mine, Bob, and I were returning from a lunch meeting in New York City. As we crossed a street, I noticed a bill on the pavement. As I picked it up I saw it was a twenty-dollar bill. I turned to Bob and said, "Wow, who finds a twenty-dollar bill nowadays?" As we continued to walk across the street, a hot dog vendor stationed halfway up the next block came walking hurriedly towards us. By the time we reached the other side of the street, he began shouting in broken English, "That's my money, that's my money." With that, I shoved the bill in my pants pocket and said, "What money?"

The vendor just stopped in his tracks, turned around and went back to his waiting hot dog stand without saying another word. Bob was amazed and acknowledged that the twenty-dollar bill wasn't his. At that, I said I knew it wasn't his and that he was just trying to take advantage of the situation. He didn't even say it was a twenty. With that, this guy from the suburbs said, "I guess I would have given it to him." I then turned to Bob and said, "Yes, I know, but you're not from Brooklyn!"

CHAPTER FIFTEEN

A Wonderful, Wonderful Adventure

There were so many wonderful places that were part of lives in the 1950's and 60's. To me, the mere thought of some of them conjures up sweet memories. Some of these places are long gone from the Brooklyn scene, yet others are still much alive and thriving to this day.

Coney Island was the absolute coolest place for us to go to. It was only about a two-mile walk away from my house. Summertime and the beach went hand in hand. Bay 15 was our favorite bay to put down our blankets. I remember the guys selling hot knishes from their heavily loaded backpacks as they trudged through the sand. A potato knish is basically a baked square of dough with a mashed potato filling. After eating a knish smothered in brown mustard, we'd look for the ice cream guys to pass by. It was wonderful.

We started out as toddlers, and until we were about three years old, our mothers would change us on the beach as a towel was held around us. The times were very different from today and at the early age of eleven or

James C. DeLaura

twelve, we'd be off on our own joining friends for a day at the beach. We would take the train or save the carfare for treats we'd buy during the day. It's hard to believe we were allowed to be on our own at such an early age, but times were really different and we all knew to stay together when there. We all were pretty good swimmers and enjoyed the saltwater as we body surfed and built sandcastles along the shore. One of my cousins reminds me of my "desert soldier routine" where I would crawl over the sand as if I had been marooned on a desert for days. Crying for water, I would sometimes lay face down only to rise up with sand stuck to my skin. Once one of them gave me water, I would stop acting the part. I'm sure I stopped playing this game once I discovered girls. Somehow, I didn't think they would be too impressed with it. When it rained, or we were caught in some passing storm, we would all huddle under the boardwalk to wait it out. I remember the cool sand under my feet as we stood with towels over our shoulders to keep warm – all the time praying we would not be struck by some lightning bolt flashing through the spaces between the boardwalk's wooden slats. Sometimes, the storm would

James C. DeLaura

pass and we'd resume play on the beach. If not, we'd pack up and go home, all of us looking like we'd been through the wringer. It really didn't matter to us as we all knew there was always another day at the beach just around the corner.

Spending the day in Coney Island also meant the possibility of going on rides. With money being tight, we would be very selective of the rides we'd go on. One of the favorites was a large Carousel. This was more than the usual kiddie merry-go-round. It went pretty fast and the one feature you couldn't forget was the catching of the rings. The operator would load a bunch of steel rings, about the size of a silver dollar into a wooden arm that he would tilt into the carousel's path of travel. It was kept back about three feet and the riders on the outside horses would lean out with an extended arm to try to catch one. Every once in awhile there would be a brass ring in the mix, which if caught, would net you a free ride. Once the all rings were caught, the operator would hold out a basket so you could toss them back for the next ride. Even though some of the rings fell on the ground, he always seemed to

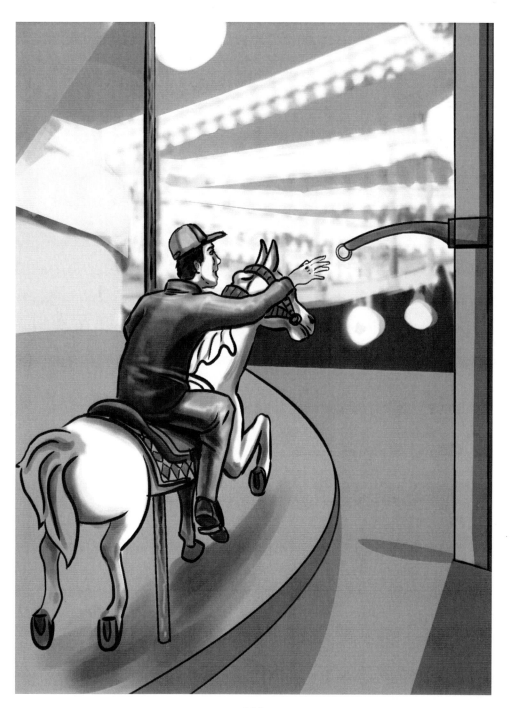

know if he didn't get all of them back. He would extend the ride a few minutes as he yelled at us to put them in his basket. Everyone wanted one for a souvenir to impress the girls and he knew it.

When back home, the summertime meant we'd see an almost endless parade of ice cream trucks, Italian ice vendors and street rides. Most of these vendors had a truck that made a distinct sound as it came down our block. Some used bells while others had music similar to what you'd hear from a loud music box. We all instantly knew which truck was there based on their specific sound. While all these treats were readily available, we were lucky to be able to get an ice cream or a ride more than once or twice a week. When we were able to earn some of our own money we could have it more often. Funny though, when it came to paying with our own money, we were less likely to spend it on ice cream that often. I suppose the little things, like having to buy our own treats or saving up for what we really wanted, contributed towards our appreciation of a dollar. In many ways, these early lessons were the basis for much of our thinking today. Why does one person seem to embrace an "I want it now" philosophy and another plans for what they want and works towards getting it? For me, growing up the way I did in Brooklyn, with all its gives and takes, set me on a more conservative path in life.

As a young adult, the hustle and bustle of building a responsible life didn't leave much, if any, time to reminisce about my childhood experiences. Staying focused on family and career matters was all too important. It's only since retirement have I been able to look back with such enthusiasm. Now, it's my sons that are the young adults that are having children and focusing on family and career. It's the circle of life we all talk about, and it is real life. With the years still ahead of me I feel blessed and fortunate to be able to share in some of the developing memories of my children. As my sons encouraged me to write this book of my Brooklyn past, perhaps they, too, will someday write a book of their own. Sharing my stories has been a privilege for me. I hope they were a joy to you as well as an inspiration for you to remember and enjoy your own stories. Looking back, I can honestly say it's been a wonderful, wonderful adventure.

POSTSCRIPT

POSTSCRIPT

To me, "Stories From A Brooklyn Stoop," really has no end. Additional chapters can be written by just about anyone who was raised in this wonderful country of ours. Whether these memories took shape on a stoop, porch, or park bench, they belong to us individually. I feel so fortunate to have been able to write this book about my stories to share with you. However, I cannot shake loose the notion that so many people will never have the same opportunity to share their memories as I have. This includes all that have lost their lives in defense of our country and our way of life.

Years before living through many of the experiences I've written about, the impacts of a world fraught with conflict weighed heavily on me as well as the rest of America. My first recollection of the fear of war came about when I was a young Brooklyn teenager. The Atomic Age and the Cuban Missile Crisis of 1962 loomed over all of us every day. It was the first time my friends and I were old enough to truly understand the gravity of the situation the whole country and the world was facing. When the war in Vietnam took so many lives, I wrote a poem to express how I was feeling. The poem was about a dream I wished would come true someday. All too often, over the past decades, I would ask the questions posed in that poem and felt so sad that they still remained unanswered.

Just A Dream?

Dream my friends of this mad endeavor,
To end all wars forever and ever,
Never to see another man die,
A woman suffer, or a child cry,
Is it madness for us to scheme,
Why does it have to be just a dream?

Now, as a grandparent, I look at life with a renewed sense of hope that one day this dream will be a reality for all of us. Whether it's their own stories from a Brooklyn stoop, or their countryside front porch – our children, grandchildren and the generations to come deserve to have their own good memories.

ACKNOWLEDGMENTS

ACKNOWLEDGMENTS

My wife, Joanne, my best friend and love of my life, you have supported me every step of the way as I wrote "Stories From A Brooklyn Stoop." You inspired me to press on and complete my memoir about a glorious time in my life. Reading my drafts, listening to excerpts and offering your sound advice was crucial to my writing. I can never thank you enough for being there for me.

Loving parents nurture their children to prepare them for their life's journey. It's a wonderful experience when their children show them the same caring support in return. I feel blessed to have such loving sons and daughters-in-law who have rallied to support me as the stories of my book came together.

To my sons, Christopher and Matthew, you both became my personal cheerleaders with your relentless encouragement to finish my book. You helped keep me moving forward as I wrote about my boyhood in Brooklyn. As I have always valued your opinions and suggestions, you both came through for me once again. Thank you, Chris and Matt - the pride you exhibit in me makes me feel like the luckiest father in the world.

My daughters-in-law, Mita and Vy, you were very supportive as my stories came to life. Whenever I sought your counsel, you both applied your unique interpersonal and educational skills to enhance the effectiveness of my written word. In essence, you became my first-line editors. I can't say enough to express my appreciation to the both of you.

Many of my other family members played important roles as advisors, sources of information, or inspiration for me. To my sister, Lilly, and brother-in-law, Larry, thank you both for your enthusiastic help in gathering photos and fact checking some family history. I will always remember the smiles on your faces as I shared some of our stories from the past.

To you, my dear cousins, Rozzie and Jim, I relish in the knowledge that you both have fond memories of our youth growing up in the old neighborhood. I thank both of you for your encouragement and for sharing some of those stories with me. It made writing my book all the more rewarding.

One of the highlights of writing a book about my youth was discussing it with two of my dear aunts. Thank you, Aunt Rita and Aunt Jean, for your help with vintage photos and historical information about our family. You both are not only links to my past, but will always be a loving part of my life. Thank you again.

Besides my wonderful family, I am so happy to still enjoy a close relationship with one of my childhood friends. Jim, you've been my best friend for nearly 60 years and have always been special to me. As you know, many of my stories are really our stories. Thank you for your support related to the book, but more so for playing a dear part in my life.

I would also like to thank "Russell Brands, LLC, owner of the SPALDING® and SPALDEEN® registered trademarks. They were gracious enough to respond to my inquiries in regards to using their name when recounting some of the games that we played as kids and the balls that we used.

The creative team at Penforhirenyc (penforhirenyc.com) was instrumental in helping to make this vision a reality. And for that I want to thank Matthew Harms for his consultation on this project, which included editing, page layout, formatting and getting it through to the final stage of publishing. A big thank you also to Mike

McKenna who designed the book cover and brought some of the artwork on the interior pages to life.

My thanks to Lou Gallo (lougallo.com) for his help in creating the initial artwork based on my recollection of the games I played and experiences I had as a boy in the 1950's and 60's.

The creative talents of VOX Illustrations, a custom illustration agency (voxillustration.com) provided many of the finished images used in the book. My thanks go out to my project manager, Ben Rogers, and his design team.

Made in United States
North Haven, CT
14 January 2024

47451264R00188